THE LARDER INVADED.

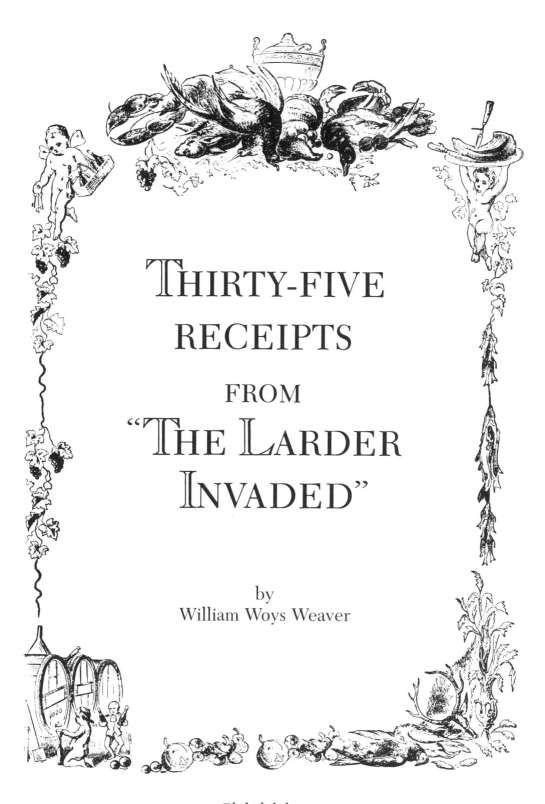

Thirty-five Receipts

from

"The Larder Invaded"

by
William Woys Weaver

Philadelphia
The Library Company of Philadelphia
The Historical Society of Pennsylvania
1986

Library of Congress Catalog Card No. 86-082602
ISBN 0-914-07669-8

Printed By
The Winchell Company of Philadelphia

Foreword

This collection of recipes is drawn from materials assembled for the exhibition "The Larder Invaded: Reflections on Three Centuries of Philadelphia Food and Drink" presented jointly by the Library Company of Philadelphia and the Historical Society of Pennsylvania. It is intended as a gustatory guide through the exhibit—small tastings, if you will, of the huge feast that has unfolded from Philadelphia's culinary past. We hope that this tasting will offer a broad range of perspectives on Philadelphia and its cookery, from soup kitchens to the luxuries of caramel ice cream. Each recipe is a story in itself; all are stories within the story that weave themselves together in one fascinating culinary plot in which the only villain is temptation, and that quickly forgiven.

Ours would be a perfect party if we could give these cookbooks as gifts to all the visitors to our exhibit, but alas, realities dictate that we must set a price. On the bright side, income from our *Thirty-Five Receipts* will go to the fund that has made the exhibition possible. By purchasing this little collection, you have also supported the effort. We are deeply grateful to you and sincerely hope that you use and enjoy the recipes gathered here for your pleasure. They are part of a heritage that belongs not only to Philadelphia, America's first culinary capital, but to all America.

> John C. Van Horne
> Librarian
> Library Company of Philadelphia
>
> Peter J. Parker
> Director
> Historical Society of Pennsylvania

Introduction

"The Larder Invaded" is a picture, a hand-tinted lithograph, published by Philadelphian William Smith, depicting a cat and dog raiding their master's larder of elegantly hung game. Metaphorically, the dog and cat may represent Adam and Eve savoring the culinary spoils of Eden, for certainly the eighteenth and nineteenth century Philadelphia larder was a culinary Eden of sorts. However, we prefer to apply this metaphor more directly to ourselves, that is, to The Library Company of Philadelphia and the Historical Society of Pennsylvania, whose bibliographic larders are beyond question a scholar's Paradise, and for the lover of food, a complete revelation not unlike Eve's apple.

As it happened, her apple turned out to be a very large one. Over a brown-bag lunch two years ago, I chatted about my projected work on a history of Philadelphia foods. The expected "handful" of cooking buffs swelled into a respectable crowd. The turnout was evidence enough that an exhibit on Philadelphia foods and foodways would be the only natural next step. Thus prodded, we plumbed the collections of the two institutions to see what they had to offer in a culinary way.

The outcome brings us back to the image of Eve's apple, yet our only original sin was the unnecessary fear (or presumption) that surely there would not be enough for a show. The patient siftings of the Library Company's Mary Anne Hines, Gordon Marshall, and Sally Jo Sorensen cast out our fears completely: the Philadelphia larder it seems was indeed a very full one. Thus, we can now honestly boast that our exhibit, which takes its name from the old lithograph, is but the first foray into the rich larders of these two institutions.

This cookbook skims the surface of those gleanings. It is a selection of recipes that represents different aspects of food treated in the exhibit. It is also a companion volume to the exhibition catalogue, which condenses the story into handy reference size. Like the catalogue, one can carry the cookbook through the exhibit and actually examine the original source—or others like it in nearby cases, see the type of equipment that may have been used to make the dish, and, with the help of the tested version of the recipe, reproduce the food at home. It is our intention that food history be living history, where eating and learning give savor to revelation.

Bonnes récherches, bon appétit!
William Woys Weaver,
Guest Curator

Note to the Reader

Throughout this cookbook, where directions call for chopping, mincing, slicing, or pureeing, the recipes were tested with the Cuisinart DLC-X Plus for large batches and the DLC-10 Plus for small. We are grateful to Cuisinarts for making this equipment available to us. It is possible to reproduce many of the textures peculiar to historic cookery with modern equipment. We suggest that you follow our directions closely in this regard, and for professional accuracy, use a kitchen scale to weigh dry ingredients rather than "guesstimate" with cups.

Table of Contents

CARROT PUDDING

[1699]

SOURCE: ANNE TOLLER.

Her Book Given by Mrs. Hall in the Year 1699. *MS*.

[England, 1699], page 13.

ROUGHWOOD COLLECTION.

We have chosen this recipe for two reasons. First, Anne Toller's cookbook represents the type of household record that was brought to Pennsylvania by early families of means. It represents the cookery of the gentry rather than that of the middle class.[1] In this respect, Anne Toller's recipes compare favorably with Gulielma Penn's (see recipe 2).

Secondly, the Toller manuscript contains a great many recipes worthy of note to historians of Anglo-American foods and foodways. For example, Mrs. Toller records a recipe for King William's breakfast cake (perhaps unique), a recipe for "Wafers ye Dutch way" (by which she meant waffles), an early recipe for chocolate cream (we would call it chocolate mousse today), not to mention her exquisite carrot pudding. Only after reading Amelia Simmons' sparse recipe for carrot pudding in *American Cookery* (Hartford, 1796) can we begin to appreciate what the New England experience did to the cookery of baroque England. In Pennsylvania, however, recipes of this sort waxed richer instead of leaner on the tables of the Quaker grandees.

The pudding is fairly easy to make once the idiosyncrasies of Mrs. Toller's language are overcome; she wrote it out the way she *said* it. We have, however, found two discrepancies in the course of testing: the egg whites are left out first, but must go back in last (a procedure we found typical of other recipes from the period); and there is about twice the necessary amount of butter—personal taste perhaps, oily inevitably. We suggest 6 oz. for better structural balance. This translates into better texture.

---

[1]A useful study of this subject is Peter Brears, *The Gentlewoman's Kitchen: Great Food in Yorkshire 1650-1750* (Wakefield, England: Wakefield Historical Publications, 1984.)

To make a Carrot pudding,

Take some of ye best Carrots boyle y^m tender pulp y^m through a Corce sive then wheigh a pound & half of ye pulp put to it half a pound of Corrans 3 quarters of a pound of butter six eggs leave out ye whites sweeten it to your tast wth fine suger & put in some grated nutmeg & a little salt butter your dish & set it into an oven quick but not two hot 3 quarters of an hour will bake it or less

2 lbs. carrots, pared, trimmed and
  cooked
6 oz. butter
¾ cup sugar
1 tblsp. nutmeg

1 tsp. salt
6 eggs, yolks and whites separated
8 oz. currants

Cook the carrots in 2 cups of water (or steam them, which is better) and drain. Puree as fine as possible in a food processor; then add the butter, sugar, nutmeg, and salt. When this cools, beat the egg yolks to a cream and fold into the batter. Add the currants. Beat the egg whites to a stiff froth. Fold them in and pour the batter into a buttered baking dish roughly 9 x 13 x 2 inches in size. Bake 45 minutes at 350°F.

NOTE: This is best when served at room temperature soon after baking. The longer the pudding stands after it has cooled, the heavier it will become. Whipped cream sweetened with sugar and orange flower water is appropriate as a topping.

GOOSEBERRY MARMALADE

[1702]

SOURCE: GULIELMA SPRINGETT PENN.

"My Mother's Recaipts for Cookerys Presarving and Chyrurgery—William Penn," *[Worminghurst, England, 1702].* In: *Miscellaneous MSS. of William Penn Vol. 6, page 79.*

HISTORICAL SOCIETY OF PENNSYLVANIA.

Recipe of Gulielma Springett Penn (1644-1694), first wife of William Penn.

According to the research of Evelyn Benson, the Penn family receipt book from which this recipe is taken was transcribed in 1702 by Edward Blackfan, a member of the Penn household at Worminghurst. The transcription was made for William Penn, Jr., evidently in preparation for his trip to Pennsylvania. Since Rebecca Blackfan, Edward's widow, became a caretaker at Pennsbury in 1713, there is little doubt that the cookbook was actually put to use in Pennsylvania.[1]

Too make gosbery Marmalett

put the gosberys in a pot or mugg and sett them one boyling watter Lett the freuit bee very soft then put them in a Coulander, and Lett the Liquor & substance Run from them, then take 3 or 4 of youre grenest Apells, pare and cutt them in thin slices and Strain them too the gosberys past then take as much sugar as the pap doth way and boyle it to a Candy Hight

This is a charming marmalade with an unusual and attractive texture. We have chosen it because we would be remiss as historians of Philadelphia food if we omitted a recipe from the proprietor's household, but also because the gooseberry was king in early Pennsylvania kitchen gardens. Genteel households boasted not one, but several different varieties, and period cookbooks abounded in recipes using them, from whips and marmalades to pies and water ices. On a practical level, before the age of Sure-Jell, gooseberries provided a source of pectin, thus giving cooks in June and July what quinces supplied in October and November.

---

[1]For a full account of the cookbook and its publication, see Evelyn A. Benson, *Penn Family Recipes* (York, Pa.: George Shumway, 1966).

The strategy of Guli's recipe is simple: rather than cooking the berries to shreds, they are suspended, deflated but still whole, in a candied apple puree, and a clever idea it is. To bring the recipe down to modern terms, we suggest the following procedure.

1 lb. ripe gooseberries
3-4 tart green apples, or enough to yield 8 oz. of puree
sugar

Remove the stems and tails of the berries. Rinse and drain thoroughly. Set the berries in a small preserving pan, and place this in a large kettle of boiling water. Or, set the berries in a vegetable steamer over 1 cup of water, and cover. Cook until the fruit is soft. Set a colander over a bowl; pour the berries into the colander and drain. Reserve 1 cup of the juice. If using a vegetable steamer, remove the basket and let the berries cool. Reserve 1 cup of water from the bottom of the steamer.

Pare, core, and slice the apples, and cook them until soft in the cup of reserved water from the berries. When soft, puree the apples and liquid together in a blender or food processor. Weigh out 8 ounces; then combine this with the berries. Weigh the fruit mixture and weigh out an equal quantity of sugar. Heat the sugar in the oven set at 250°F. Bring the fruit to a gentle boil, add the hot sugar, and boil hard until it begins to jell. Put up in hot, sterilized jelly glasses, and seal. Yield: approximately five cups.

NOTE: The apples Guli Penn calls for should provide no difficulty here, as "coddlings" were clearly intended—coddlings being the old term for cooking apples. Small, tart Greenings were the standard June and July coddlings—the 17th and 18th century type weighing 2-3 ounces apiece before paring which neatly fits the number of apples required in the original recipe.

« 3 »

ARTICHOKE HEARTS IN CREAM SAUCE
[1734]

SOURCE: JOHN MIDDLETON.

Five Hundred New Receipts. *London: Printed for Thomas Astley, 1734, page 38.*

LIBRARY COMPANY OF PHILADELPHIA.

Recipe of John Middleton, cook to the Duke of Bolton, as revised and recommended by Henry Howard (fl. 1703-1729), variously cook to the Duke of Ormond, the Earl of Salisbury and the Earl of Winchelsea.

Anyone who gardens in Pennsylvania knows very well that globe artichokes require a much longer growing season than Nature has allotted the region. Nonetheless, globe artichokes appeared from time to time on the tables of the wealthy throughout the colonial period. They were a troublesome and expensive vegetable, but since they are one of the few that actually improves from standing a few days after picking, in all probability artichokes traveled to Philadelphia via coastal sloops from points south, or else from local orangeries. In any case, we have chosen this recipe because it is both elegant in 18th century terms and representative of the "white gravy" cookery that was so popular in Philadelphia before the Revolution. Ultimately, white gravy made its way across the American landscape into far-flung parts of the country—not always with the best culinary results, but extensively enough to be associated with a whole generation of cookery by the late 19th century.[1] As in the case of this artichoke recipe, white gravy cookery owes much of its technique to the fricassee, or to some permutation of it.

To dress Artichokes with Cream

"Boil your Artichokes, then toss them up in butter in a Stew-pan; put to them some Cream, Chives, and Parsley; thicken your Sauce with the Yolk of an Egg, and put in some Salt and a little Nutmeg; serve them on small Dishes or Plates."

---

[1]William Woys Weaver, "White Gravies in American Popular Diet," in: *Food in Change* (Edinburgh: John Donald, 1986), p. 41-52.

Five Hundred
NEW RECEIPTS

IN

COOKERY,

CONFECTIONARY,

PASTRY,

PRESERVING,

CONSERVING,

PICKLING;

AND THE

Several Branches of thefe ARTS necessary to be known by all good HOUSEWIVES.

By *JOHN MIDDLETON,*

Cook to his Grace the late Duke of *Bolton.*

Revifed and Recommended by

Mr. *HENRY HOWARD.*

THOMAS ASTLEY.

LONDON.

Printed for THO. ASTLEY, at the *Rofe* againft the North Door of St. *Paul*'s.

M DCC XXXIV.

---

3. This copy belonged to James Coxe, a drawing teacher in Philadelphia, whose books were purchased by the Library Company in 1832.

To prepare this in your own kitchen, take:

8 artichokes (one per person)
1 lemon, sliced
3 tblsp. butter
1 cup heavy whipping cream
1 tsp. chives, minced
1½ tsp. parsley, minced
1 egg yolk
½ tsp. nutmeg
salt to taste (no more than ¼ tsp.)

Rinse and drain the artichokes. Trim off the tough outer petals, and the top ⅓ of each head, as shown in the woodcut (left). Remove the center or flower and rinse off any spiny material. Drain upside down until ready to cook. Set four at a time in approximately 1 gallon of boiling water with 1 sliced lemon and poach until tender. Drain upside down until free of all excess water.

Melt the butter in a broad saucepan and toss the prepared hearts until they begin to brown very slightly. Remove from the pan, and arrange on individual warm plates. Beat the yolk and cream together, and add to the pan. Add the chives and parsley, and stir gently until a thick sauce forms. Season and fill each artichoke with sauce. Pour the excess sauce around the artichokes and garnish with a sprinkle of minced chives. Excellent as a side dish with fish.

CHEESECAKE THE COMMON WAY
[1791]

SOURCE: FRIEDERIKE LÖFFLER.

Oekonomisches Handbuch für Frauenzimmer. *Stuttgart: Johann Christoph Betulius, 1791, page 456.*

LIBRARY COMPANY OF PHILADELPHIA.

The German element was an influential one in Philadelphia well into the latter half of the 19th century. In many areas of food production, such as bread and biscuit baking, the manufacture of chocolate and mustard, butchering, and tavernkeeping, the Germans reigned supreme. However, love of cheesecake was shared by both English and German-speaking Philadelphians, and early in the 18th century, this love became something of a local cult at The Cheesecake House.

Situated on the west side of 4th Street, on grounds extending from Cherry Street to Apple Tree Alley, the Cheesecake House stood in the middle of a pleasure garden shaded by cherry and apple trees, dotted with arbors and gazebos for dining *al fresco*. Even in 1848, nearly a century after it had disappeared, the Cheesecake House was still fondly remembered in the *Sunday Dispatch*.[1] We cannot recreate the Cheesecake House of the 1730s, but we can recreate one of the most popular cheesecake recipes from the German community in the city.

It comes from Friederike Löffler's classic Swabian cookbook, which was imported and sold throughout the Pennsylvania-German community.[2] In the 1850s, the cookbook was finally published in Philadelphia under the title *Vollständiges Kochbuch für die Deutsch-Amerikanische Küche* (Complete Cookbook for the German-American Kitchen) with the cheesecake recipe virtually unchanged.[3]

---

[1][Philadelphia] *Sunday Dispatch*, Aug. 27, 1848.
[2]See William Woys Weaver, *Sauerkraut Yankees* (Philadelphia: University of Pennsylvania Press, 1983), p. 8-10.
[3]For bibliographical material on this cookbook, see William Woys Weaver, "Additions and Corrections to Lowenstein's Bibliography of American Cookery Books, 1742-1860," *Proceedings of the American Antiquarian Society*, (1983) 92:2, p. 373-377.

Käßkuchen auf gewöhnliche Art.

Man rührt einen zarten sauren Käß eine Zeitlang in einer Schüssel, thut gleich eine Handvoll weis Mehl daran, dann 2 Eyer, einen Vierling verlassenen Butter, ein wenig Salz, ein paar Löffel Rosenwasser und eine Handvoll gewaschene kleine Rosinen dazu. Wann diß untereinander gerührt ist, wird die Masse auf einem von Butter- oder aufgeriebenem Taig verfertigten Kuchen gleich ausgebreitet, der Kuchen ein wenig mit verlassenem Butter begossen und gebaken.

Cheesecake the Common Way
(Translation)

Work a soft, sharp cheese in a deep mixing bowl for awhile [until smooth.] Then add a handful of fine cake flour, then two eggs, a "Vierling" of melted butter, a little salt, a few tablespoons of rosewater, and a handful of cleaned currants. Once this is folded together, spread the mixture in a prepared pie crust of puff paste or crumb dough. Pour a little melted butter over the cake and bake.

1 lb. sharp soft cheese	4 oz. melted butter
3 tblsp. flour	2 tblsp. rosewater
2 eggs	3 heaping tblsp. currants

NOTE: To recreate the type of aged soft cheese used by the Pennsylvania Germans in the 18th century, combine 4 oz. of French Boucheron (without rind) with 12 oz. *natural* cream cheese. For the latter, we recommend the cream cheese available from Fleur de Lait Foods, New Holland, Pennsylvania 17557, sold under the brand name "Quaker" cream cheese or a similar product.

Work the two cheeses together until smooth; then beat the eggs to a froth and work them into the cheese. Add the flour and melted butter and beat smooth. Fold in the currants, and lastly, add the rosewater.

Spread the mixture evenly in a prepared 10-inch pie shell of puff pastry or crumb paste. Press the filling down gently to be certain it has completely filled the shell. Bake at 350°F for one hour.

Crumb Paste

1 cup ground almonds	1¾ cups cake flour
2 egg yolks	¼ tsp. salt
4 oz. butter	3 tblsp. rum or brandy

Rub the butter, flour, and salt to a fine crumb; then combine with the ground almonds. Make a hole in the center and add the egg yolks. Add the rum or brandy and stir until the yolk/rum mixture is smooth; then gradually work this into the crumbs until a soft dough is formed. Roll out and line the baking dish. Prick the bottom and fill the shell as directed above.

NOTE: There is *no sugar* in this cheesecake. It is meant to be eaten with very sweet jam or jelly spread over the top. Pineapple honey or stewed quinces are particularly elegant when served as a topping.

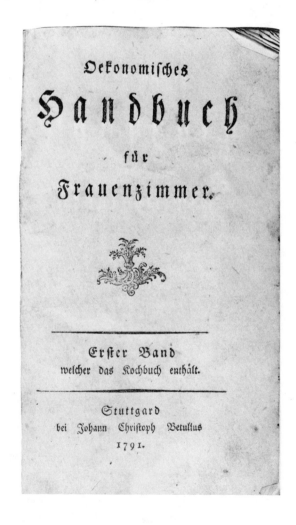

4. Unrecorded edition, before the "First Edition."

PICKLED RED CABBAGE

⟦ 1792 ⟧

SOURCE: **RICHARD BRIGGS.**

The New Art of Cookery. *Philadelphia: W. Spotswood,*
R. Campbell, and B. Johnson, 1792, page 509.

LIBRARY COMPANY OF PHILADELPHIA.

The importance of Richard Briggs' *New Art of Cookery* has been much
overlooked. Along with John Farley's *London Art of Cookery,* his cookbook is one
of the cornerstones of professional cooking as practiced in Philadelphia during the
Federal Period. Briggs' book was first issued in 1788 in London, where he was chef
at the Temple Coffee-House. At least two more American editions appeared in 1798
—one in Philadelphia, the other in Boston—which should suggest to us that
Briggs was more than a passing fancy. His ice cream recipes were certainly
prototypes for the development of the Philadelphia article. We were charmed,
however, by his pickled red cabbage, perhaps because it makes such a delightful
and typical period side dish, or perhaps because it fits so well into a venison dinner,
and does not work at cross purposes with porter.

Red Cabbage

Slice the cabbage very fine cross-ways, put it on an earthen dish, sprinkle
a handful of salt over it, cover it with another dish, and let it stand
twenty-four hours; then put it in a cullender to drain, and lay it in your
jar; take white wine vinegar enough to cover it, a little cloves, mace, and
all-spice; put them in whole, with one pennyworth of cochineal bruised
fine; boil it up and put it over the cabbage hot or cold, which you like
best, cover it close with a cloth till it is cold, and then tie it over with
leather.

We suggest cutting the original recipe in half, as follows:

3½ lb. red cabbage	¼ tsp. whole cloves
1 oz. sea salt or pickling salt	½ tblsp. mace, in clove or shredded form
2⅓ cups of red wine vinegar	½ tsp. whole allspice
1 cup spring water (use bottled water if necessary)	1 cup white sugar (optional)

Shred the cabbage paper-thin and put it in a pot or crock, scattering salt between
layers of the cabbage. Cover the pot, and let stand overnight. In the morning,
drain the cabbage, but *do not rinse.*

Bring the vinegar to a boil, add the spring water, sugar (optional), and spices. Boil hard for four minutes. Put the cabbage in a clean crock and pour the boiling vinegar mixture over it. (We used a three-gallon salt-glazed crock.) Press the cabbage down so that it is completely covered with vinegar. Cover and set away in a cold place, such as an unheated pantry or the refrigerator. Use as needed. This was originally treated as a salad.

NOTE: It was customary to cut the acidity in vinegar with water, since pickling vinegars were once made much sharper than today. This does not necessarily mean that modern taste is prepared for the sourness of old-style pickles, so we suggest adding a cup of sugar. The use of red wine vinegar will eliminate the need to redden the pickle as directed with cochineal (a dead insect). The use of tap water (which is chemically treated) will destabilize any old pickle recipe, and should therefore be avoided. If made strictly as directed above, this cabbage will keep at least five months. Be certain, of course, that you have thoroughly scalded the crock before filling it, and that the contents are kept covered and free of dust, pets, or what have you.

FRICASSEE OF PIGEONS, THE ITALIAN WAY
[1796]

SOURCE: HANNAH GLASSE.

The Art of Cookery Made Plain and Easy. *London: Printed for T. Longman, 1796, page 119.*

LIBRARY COMPANY OF PHILADELPHIA.

Things made in the Italian style were very much in vogue among fashion-conscious Philadelphians during the period of the early Republic. Italian fireworks, paintings, music by Cimarosa, frescoes and water ices bubble up with Latin frivolity from the pages of early city newspapers. As we have suggested in our introduction to the exhibition catalogue (the companion volume to this cookbook), there is something to be said for the similarities between old Philadelphia and Venice. We have continued that theme in this recipe because it makes excellent thematic eating, and because squab and its wild cousins were considered classics in the hands of Philadelphia cooks.

If the urbane reader suspects Mrs. Glasse of taking liberties with Italian cookery, we shall be the first to acknowledge it, on this condition: "The Italian Way" did not mean literally "as the Italians do it" but rather as the English *imagined* they did it. Such evocative recipe exotica made fashionable reference to Grand Tour dining in the Veneto, Palladian villas, and all the other images that the English gentry had of Italy. By osmosis through English books and English cooks, such impressions were planted in distant American minds.

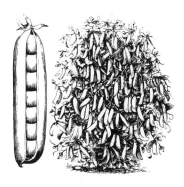

To fricassee Pigeons the Italian Way

Quarter them, and fry them in oil; take some green peas and let them fry in the oil till they are almost ready to burst, then put some boiling water to them; season it with salt, pepper, onions, garlic, parsley, and vinegar. Veal and lamb do the same way, and thicken with yolks of eggs.

We will also allow that this is not very clear as to quantity. We have tested it with sufficient ingredients for four servings.

LE PIGEON GROSSE-GORGE ENFLEE.

2 squabs, quartered
¼ cup olive oil
1 lb. 4 oz. fresh green peas, cooked
1 cup boiling water or broth made
 from the squab giblets
salt and pepper
10 oz. onion, chopped fine
 (approx. 1½ cups)
3 tsp. minced garlic, more or less
2 egg yolks, beaten
1 tblsp. fresh parsley, minced
1 tblsp. sherry vinegar

Quarter the squabs. Fry in oil until tender. Remove, drain the oil, and reserve 1 tablespoonful. Do not clean the pan. Add the onion, garlic, and reserved oil and fry gently until the onion is soft. Add the boiling water or broth, thicken with the egg yolks; then add the squab. Cover, and simmer five minutes; then add the peas, which should be previously cooked. Adjust the seasonings and add the vinegar. Garnish with minced parsley, and serve hot on a large platter with the squab in the middle and the peas in a wreath around them.

NOTE: Mrs. Glasse fries her peas, which would work with old-style peas (because they were tougher and required longer cooking). Modern varieties are bred for quick cooking, and are thus better when done separately. Otherwise, they may go to mush before the fricassee is ready to serve. Incidentally, the vinegar is not intended to make the fricassee sour, but to make the peas sweeter. The garlic should suggest a warm background flavor, not an overwhelming one, thus absolute quantity will depend on the strength of the garlic used.

GOOD MEAT SOUP

[1800]

SOURCE: WILLIAM HENRY CAVENDISH BENTINCK, Third Duke of Portland.

Copy of a Letter from the Duke of Portland, to the Lord Lieutenant of the County of Chester . . . For the Purpose of Alleviating the Distresses of the Poor. *Chester, England: Printed by J. Fletcher, 1800, page 13.*

ROUGHWOOD COLLECTION.

The first soup kitchen in the city was established at the corner of 6th and Cherry Streets in 1803 by the Female Association of Philadelphia. According to their constitution, they modeled their efforts on earlier soup kitchens in England, among them the Duke of Portland's plan.[1] Since the soup kitchen became an unfortunate necessity in dealing with urban poverty, and since such cookery is rarely touched upon in cookbooks, we have thrust our hand into the pot, so to speak, and come up with the Duke's recipe. The real surprise came later when we tested it: the soup lives up to its name in all respects.

Ingredients necessary to make 100 gallons of Good Meat Soup, Winchester measure, according to the scale adopted in Orchard-street, Westminster; with a specification of the expences of each article according to the present prices.

			£.	s.	d.
Meat {	112lb. legs and shins of beef, 2d. - - -		0	18	8
	63lb. Clods and stickings ditto, 3½d. - -		0	18	4½
	175lb. average price 2¼d. per lb. - - -	£.	1	17	0½
Split peas	18 - - - - - - - - -	4d.	0	6	0
Barley	30 - - - - - - - - -	3d.	0	7	6
Onions	18 - - - - - - - - -	1¼d.	0	1	10½
Salt	8 - - - - - - - - -	2¾d.	0	1	10
Pepper	10 oz. - - - - - -	1¾d.	0	1	5½
Total	149lb. 10 oz. of ingredients - - -	£.	2	15	8½
Coals, about 1¼ bushel - - - - - - - -			0	1	6½
			£. 2	17	3

---

[1]*The Constitution of the Female Association of Philadelphia* (Philadelphia: Jane Aitken, 1803), p. 16-17.

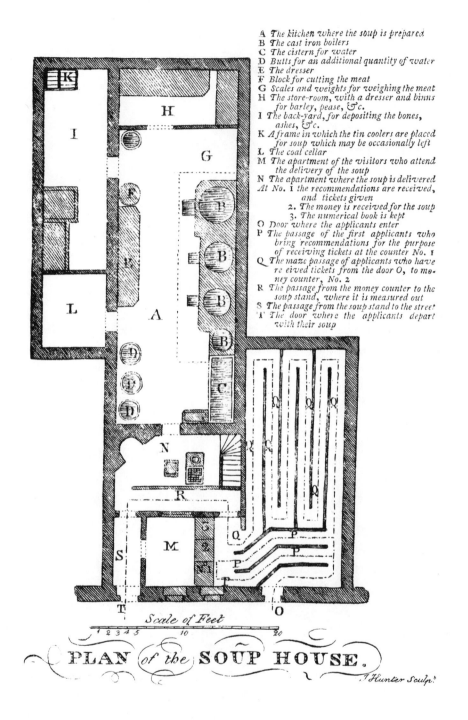

A The kitchen where the soup is prepared
B The cast iron boilers
C The cistern for water
D Butts for an additional quantity of water
E The dresser
F Block for cutting the meat
G Scales and weights for weighing the meat
H The store-room, with a dresser and binns for barley, pease, &c.
I The back-yard, for depositing the bones, ashes, &c.
K A frame in which the tin coolers are placed for soup which may be occasionally left
L The coal cellar
M The apartment of the visitors who attend the delivery of the soup
N The apartment where the soup is delivered
At No. 1 the recommendations are received, and tickets given
      2. The money is received for the soup
      3. The numerical book is kept
O Door where the applicants enter
P The passage of the first applicants who bring recommendations for the purpose of receiving tickets at the counter No. 1
Q The maze passage of applicants who have received tickets from the door O, to money counter, No. 2
R The passage from the money counter to the soup stand, where it is measured out
S The passage from the soup stand to the street
T The door where the applicants depart with their soup

Scale of Feet

1 2 3 4 5   10   20

PLAN *of the* SOUP HOUSE.

J. Hunter Sculp.

Because the recipe is intended to make 100 gallons, we have reduced the quantities proportionally. Our procedure is based on suggestions elsewhere in the Duke's pamphlet, not that the soup is very complicated. Our recipe will feed 15 persons.

6 qts. water plus 1 cup
2¾ lb. stewing beef (weight may include half bones and half "clods" or lumps of meat)
4½ oz. split peas

7½ oz. pearl barley
4½ oz. chopped onion (roughly 1 medium onion)
2 tblsp. salt
½ tsp. pepper

If using bones with meat attached, boil two hours in the water, skimming often. Then remove the bones and meat, and cut the meat into small pieces or cubes. If using only "clods", as they were called, cut into cubes and boil two hours, skimming often but do not remove "clods". Add the onion, barley, peas, salt, and pepper. Cook 45-60 minutes, or until the barley and peas are soft. Serve with a coarse grade of rye bread or no bread at all.

NOTE: The original recipe used beef shins, which are still proper, provided they can be obtained. Historically, shins were considered worthless. Most butchers threw them out or gave them to charities.

« 8 »

VERMICELLI AND CHEESE

[1802]

SOURCE: [LEWIS FRESNAYE].

To Make Soup of Vermicelli, Maccaroni and other kinds of Paste. *Philadelphia: T.S. Manning, [ca. 1802].*

LIBRARY COMPANY OF PHILADELPHIA.

Recipe of Lewis Fresnaye, vermicelli manufacturer, 57 South Front Street, ca. 1802. A French emigré, Fresnaye was active in Philadelphia during the period 1795-1805, and is believed to have been the first manufacturer of Italian pastas in the United States.

This broadsheet was probably issued as an enclosure under the wrapping of the vermicelli cakes when sold to retail customers. Fresnaye's first recipe (under "Directions," see the illustration at right) is very similar in end result to a recipe for vermicelli soup in *New American Cookery* (New York, 1805). Italian pasta was a popular, although expensive, upperclass food in Philadelphia throughout the 18th and early 19th centuries. It was eaten as a side dish generally during hot weather, and when served with cheese, was treated as a meat substitute.

Fresnaye's success as a pasta manufacturer has been difficult to assess. We suspect that his venture was short-lived. Most of the pasta consumed in early Philadelphia was shipped from Sicily via London. For example, Robert Bass, an apothecary in Market Street advertised in the *Pennsylvania Journal* of October 5, 1774, that he had just imported on the ship *Mary and Elizabeth*, French prunes, Italian vermicelli, a few truffles and morels, new aniseed, and the best Florence olive oil in chests.

We have chosen Fresnaye's last recipe in which vermicelli is prepared "like pudding." By that he meant prepared like baked pudding, not so much in texture as in technique. Anyone who makes this will immediately recognize it as the ancestor of that ubiquitous American dish called "macaroni and cheese," only Fresnaye's recipe is infinitely better. Use homemade or freshly made vermicelli and authentic *old* parmesan cheese (it has a black rind). Grate the cheese then and there, and you will begin to see how something so very simple can be transformed into a classic. To prepare it Fresnaye style, take:

3 qts. water	1 tblsp. butter
1 lb. vermicelli broken into 1-inch pieces	6 oz. grated parmesan cheese
	4 oz. butter
1½ tsp. salt	salt and pepper

Add the salt to the water and bring to a rolling boil. Add the tablespoon of butter, then the broken vermicelli. Boil gently until tender (*al dente*). Drain, but do not rinse in cold water. Lightly butter a shallow, 9 x 14 inch baking dish, fill it with the vermicelli, and pat it down evenly with a spoon. Spread the grated cheese over the top. Melt the butter and pour it zig-zag fashion over the cheese to distribute it evenly. Bake in an oven preheated to 375°F for 10-15 minutes, or until the cheese is toasted. Yield: 8-10 servings.

NOTE: This is best served piping hot with salt and plenty of freshly grated pepper. Chopped herbs may be scattered over the top after it comes from the oven. Sweet basil is an obvious choice.

To make Soup of Vermicelli, Maccaroni and other kinds of Paste.

DIRECTIONS.

TAKE a pound or two of meat or a fowl, and boil it as usual, when the meat or fowl is sufficiently boiled, and the broth has arrived to a proper consistency, take about six cakes of the paste to a pint of broth, break them in your hands; take the meat or fowl out of the pot, and while the broth is boiling, stir the paste in with a spoon, then let it boil about eight minutes..... But if the paste is of a larger size boil it more in proportion......It is then fit for use.

It may also be made by boiling the paste in milk, or in water with a little butter, in which a little grated parmisan or other good cheese will be an addition. It is in this manner that it is very salutary and nutritive for persons of a weak stomach, and in a weak and debilitated state of body, and is much used in the Italian Hospitals. This dish may well be substituted in the place of meat especially in the hot seasons of the year, when the too great use of meat is prejudicial to the health.

It is also prepared like pudding, thus:

TAKE six pints of water and boil it with a sufficiency of salt, when boiling, stir in it one pound of paste, let it boil as above, then strain the water well off, and put the paste in a large dish, mixing therewith six ounces of grated parmisan or other good cheese; then take four ounces of good butter and melt it well in a saucer or small pot, and pour it over the paste while both are warm. It would be an improvement after all is done, to keep the dish a few minutes in a hot oven, till the butter and cheese have well penetrated the paste.

It may be rendered still more delicate by boiling the paste in milk instead of water, and put a little gravy of meat, or any other meat sauce thereon

T. S. Manning, Printer, 41, Chesnut Street, Philadelphia.

RYE COFFEE
[1819]

SOURCE: SAMUEL R. FRANKLIN.

[Recipe Book]. *MS. [Philadelphia, 1819-1825], page 3.*

HISTORICAL SOCIETY OF PENNSYLVANIA.

Recipe of Samuel R. Franklin, a teacher, Alderman, Constable and Health Commissioner in Philadelphia.

The embargo placed by President Jefferson on British vessels in 1807 resulted in a severe shortage of imported coffee. Large numbers of Americans were forced to turn to roasted rye as a coffee substitute. For many years, even after the embargo was lifted, rye coffee was known locally as "family coffee," and because of its relative cheapness, it became a standard feature of institutional cookery.

While touring the prison at Philadelphia in 1829, the English Quaker Thomas Shillitoe noted that the inmates were served rye coffee sweetened with molasses with their breakfast rations.[1] Rye coffee received a better name later in the 19th century when it was discovered that it lacked caffeine and retained some of the nutritional value of the whole grain. Certainly, it is one of the few coffees of which, if one chooses, one can eat the grounds without deleterious effect!

Since the original recipe for rye coffee is reproduced (at right) in Franklin's own hand, we suggest the following method for making it in the modern kitchen.

2 cups rye
2 cups boiling water

Pick out the black or imperfect grains. Put the rye in a deep bowl and cover with the boiling water. Infuse 6-8 minutes, then pour off the water and rinse the grain thoroughly in clean cold water, using a fine sieve. Spread the grain on a fruit dryer or a tin baking sheet. If using a baking sheet, dry the grain in a slack oven set at 200°F until the grain is dry to the bite (this should occur in approximately 1½ hours). The grain must contain no perceptible moisture or it will burst when roasted. Moisture will also affect the flavor.

---

[1]*Journal of Thomas Shillitoe.* (London, 1839), II, p. 389.

To roast the grain, set the oven at 375°F, and roast as follows: 35-40 minutes for a very mild roast, 45-50 minutes for a mild roast, 55-60 minutes for a medium roast. After an hour, the grain quickly darkens and becomes more bitter and strong when made into coffee. Personal taste will dictate roasting time. In any case, stir the grain occasionally as it is roasting to be certain that the grain is darkening evenly. If you have a coffee roaster, then use it and roast the grain as you would green coffee.

To make coffee, clean out your coffee grinder, and grind the grains to your preference. One cup of grain yields approximately 1¼ cups of ground coffee when ground extra fine. One or two tablespoons of ground rye is sufficient per serving.

Put the ground rye in a coffee pot, having measured the quantity you will need, and pour boiling water over it. Cover and boil ten minutes. Let the grounds settle, then pour the coffee through a strainer. Rye coffee is made according to the same procedure as Turkish coffee, so a little "mud" in the bottom of the cup is to be expected.

NOTE: Whole grain rye is available at most health food stores.

Rye Coffee

Take a small Quantity of clear Rye say two Quarts and carefully remove from it all small or imperfect Grains – Pour on it a quantity of boiling Water & let it remain from five or Eight Minutes. Then pour off the Hot Water & wash the Grain in cold Water three or four times changing the Water every time. Set the Grain dry and after it is completely so, burn it in the same manner as West India Coffee is generally prepared.

9. Recipe Book of Samuel R. Franklin, 1819-1825.

INDIAN POUND CAKE

[1828]

SOURCE: ELIZA LESLIE.

Seventy-Five Receipts, for Pastry, Cakes, and Sweetmeats.

Boston: Munroe and Francis, 1828, page 62.

LIBRARY COMPANY OF PHILADELPHIA.

Recipe of Mrs. Elizabeth Goodfellow (1767-1851) of the Goodfellow Cooking School, Philadelphia.

This is one of Mrs. Goodfellow's "signature" recipes that appears with great regularity in Philadelphia manuscript cookbooks. With equal regularity, it is identified as one of Mrs. Goodfellow's recipes. This comes as no surprise, since Miss Leslie's *Seventy-Five Receipts* was essentially the notebook she kept while studying under Mrs. Goodfellow in 1809 or 1810. The cake is ingenious in its use of brandy or rosewater which affects not only the gluten, but reacts chemically with the other ingredients to create a delicate new flavor. Most important, in its use of cornmeal the cake conforms to Mrs. Goodfellows' advocacy of American ingredients to create an essentially American cookery, a skill for which she was an acknowledged master.

Indian Pound Cake

Eight eggs
One pint of powdered sugar
One pint of Indian meal, sifted and half a pint of wheat flour
Half pound of butter
One nutmeg grated—and a teaspoonful of cinnamon
A glass of mixed wine and brandy

Stir the butter and sugar to a cream. Beat the eggs very light. Stir the meal and eggs, alternately, into the butter and sugar. Add the spice and liquor. Stir all well. Butter a tin pan, put in the mixture, and bake it in a moderate oven. This cake should be eaten while fresh.

This is the recipe as Mrs. Goodfellow essentially taught it. Rarely does it appear in this form, that is, with so many eggs, in the manuscript notebooks of her other students. We suspect that this is the older of two versions, that with fewer eggs being the more economy conscious, and in fact, easier to do, considering the time it took to thoroughly beat eight eggs by hand.

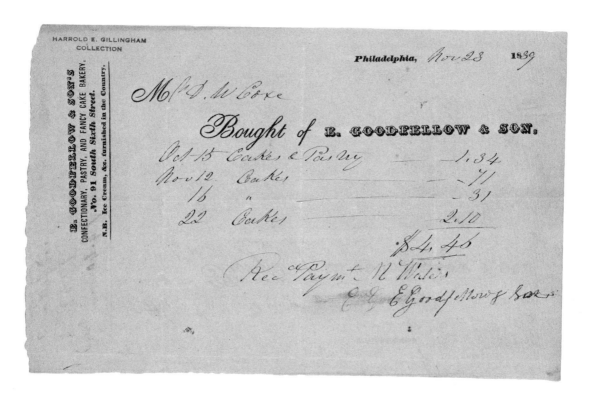

As an illustration of what happened to Mrs. Goodfellow's recipes when they "went into circulation," we offer for comparison, the Goodfellow Indian Pound Cake as it appeared in Elizabeth Ellicott Lea's *Domestic Cookery* (Baltimore, 1851), p. 116. The original manuscript for *Domestic Cookery*, which is still preserved by one of Elizabeth Lea's descendants, does not indicate from whom she obtained the recipe. But since several of her personal friends were graduates of the Goodfellow Cooking School and Miss Leslie was a friend of Andrew Ellicott's wife, Elizabeth Lea's aunt, there are certainly any number of possibilities.

Indian Pound Cake

Take three-quarters of a pound of Indian meal sifted, and one-quarter of wheat flour; roll a pound of sugar, work into it three-quarters of a pound of butter; season with nutmeg and rose brandy; add flour and eggs beaten light; mix and bake as other pound cake.

To make the cake according to Elizabeth Lea's plan, we must take into account that most commercial cornmeal is today ground differently (and less nutritionally) than in the early 19th century. In short, we will use too much if we are true to her weights as stated; one to two ounces of cornmeal must be subtracted from each pound of processed cornmeal—there is some variation here depending on the way it is ground. This rule of thumb will be useful in translating any old cornmeal recipe into modern terms. Unfortunately, rather than subtract cornmeal, many cookbook writers simply add baking powder to lighten things up. You will notice that there are *no chemicals* in either Mrs. Goodfellow's or Elizabeth Lea's recipe. Mrs. Goodfellow would gag before she swallowed anything with chemicals in it. Elizabeth Lea was less adamant. But both women shared an appreciation of *real* food—as opposed to all the rest. For one cake (½ the proportions given in Lea's recipe) take:

1½ cups white cornmeal, less 2 tblsp.	2 eggs
½ cup cake flour	1½ tblsp. rosewater mixed with
1 cup superfine sugar	1½ tblsp. brandy
6 oz. butter	1 tblsp. grated nutmeg

Cream the butter and sugar until light. Beat the eggs to a froth, and gradually add to the butter mixture. Sift the flour, cornmeal and grated nutmeg together twice, then fold into the batter. Add the rosewater and brandy, stir until well combined; then pour the batter into a greased cake tin (a 10-inch springform mold without a center tube is ideal). Bake at 350°F for 45-50 minutes or until the cake tests done in the center. Cool on a rack and serve. No icing is necessary.

NOTE: For the weak sisters and brothers who are terrified of cakes without chemical leaveners, 1 tsp. of baking powder will serve as your saving grace. It should be sifted twice with the flour and cornmeal. Also, the flour and cornmeal should be warmed slightly on the stove before they are used. By driving out that small amount of excess moisture, the cake will rise better in the oven.

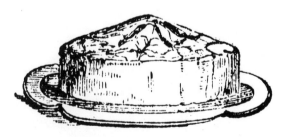

POUND CAKE.

TERRAPIN

[1843]

SOURCE: JAMES SANDERSON.

The Complete Cook. *Philadelphia: Lea & Blanchard, 1843, page 72.*

Recipe of Elizabeth Rubicam, Philadelphia cook and caterer, and co-owner—with her husband Daniel—of the Washington Hotel at 20 South 6th Street.

The Rubicams were legends in their own lifetimes for exquisite cooking and top-flight accommodations in the city. Their green turtle soup was considered the best in town, and while Daniel could claim much credit for that, it was Elizabeth who was considered by all standards of measure to be America's premier terrapin cook.[1] New York, Baltimore, and the rest of Philadelphia took their cue from her, for it was she who firmly established terrapin as a catering standby in the 19th century. So exacting was she as a cook, that her recommendation was considered testimonial enough for a new product or kitchen invention, such as the Mussey Patent Franklin Gridiron that she promoted in 1825.[2]

Eliza Leslie published Mrs. Rubicam's terrapin recipe in 1837, but without attribution.[3] James Sanderson took the matter in hand and gave credit where credit was due by identifying the recipe as Mrs. Rubicam's. That is the recipe used here.

Terrapin cookery evolved as a substitute for green turtle. Because of relentless killing, sea turtles became expensive and the market unpredictable, thus cooks turned to native species closer to home that could be adapted to green turtle cookery. It was soon discovered that terrapin had distinct qualities of its own which set it apart from snapper and sea turtle.

The best and most expensive terrapin were the Diamond Backs and Egg Harbor terrapins. The Diamond Back came from the Chesapeake, the Egg Harbor from the Delaware Bay. They differed from one another on several points of physical appearance, but not in superior flavor or texture of the meat. The males were called "bulls" and being tough, were sold by the hundred; females were tender and

---

[1] See Rubicam's advertisement in [Philadelphia] *Poulson's American Daily Advertiser,* July 7, 1819.
[2] *Philadelphia Gazette,* May 14, 1825. Mrs. Rubicam owned two of the gridirons.
[3] Eliza Leslie, *Directions for Cookery* (Philadelphia, 1837), p. 66-67.

most highly valued if they contained eggs, which were esteemed as a great delicacy. Unrestricted killing, pollution, and the draining of marshes along the bays eventually led to the demise of the terrapin. We have included Mrs. Rubicam's recipe not to encourage the turtle's extinction, but because, as Colonel John W. Forney wrote in 1879, "Terrapin is essentially a Philadelphia dish. Baltimore delights in it, Washington eats it, New York knows it; but in Philadelphia it approaches a crime not to be passionately fond of it."[4] We therefore include terrapin as a matter of historical record.

Terrapin

This is a favourite dish for suppers and parties; and, when well cooked, they are certainly very delicious. Many persons in Philadelphia have made themselves famous for cooking this article alone. Mrs. Rubicam, who during her lifetime always stood first in that way, prepared them as follows. Put the terrapins alive in a pot of boiling water, where they must remain until they are quite dead. You then divest them of their outer skin and toe-nails; and, after washing them in warm water, boil them again until they become quite tender, adding a handful of salt to the water. Having satisfied yourself of their being perfectly tender, take off the shells and clean the terrapins very carefully, removing the sand-bag and gall without breaking them. Then cut the meat and entrails into small pieces, and put into a saucepan, adding the juice which has been given out in cutting them up, but *no water*, and season with salt, cayenne, and black pepper, to your taste; adding a quarter of a pound of good butter to each terrapin, and a handful of flour for thickening. After stirring a short time, add four or five table-spoonfuls of cream, and a half pint of good Madeira to every four terrapins, and serve hot in a deep dish.

Sanderson, who was then proprietor of the Franklin House Hotel, added this footnote to the recipe:

Our own cook has been in the habit of putting in a very little mace, a large table-spoonful of mustard, and *ten drops of the gall*; and, just before serving, adding the yolks of four hard boiled eggs. During the stewing, particular attention must be paid to stirring the preparation frequently; and it must be borne in mind, that terrapins cannot possibly be too hot.

---

[4]Colonel John W. Forney, "Terrapin," *The Epicure* (New York: H.K. & F.B. Thurber Co., 1879), p. 32.

WHIPPED SYLLABUB

[1844]

SOURCE: United States Practical Receipt Book.

Philadelphia: Lindsay & Blakiston, 1844, page 239.

LIBRARY COMPANY OF PHILADELPHIA.

A number of whipped desserts went by the name of syllabub in the 17th and 18th centuries, but essentially, there were two types. One consisted of all the ingredients whipped together and "cured" overnight in a cool place (a process that also allowed the whip to drain and thicken); the other was made up light on the principle of the floating island, with the whipped ingredients bobbing atop the wine. Our recipe is one of the latter. Regardless of the method, all syllabubs were served cold in lily-shaped glasses, usually as a finale to an informal supper during hot weather, or as a part of the great wave of desserts that attacked the senses at the end of a formal dinner.

Although our recipe was published in 1844, it is much like Mrs. Hale's recipe (see recipe 13) in that it too traces to the 18th century. We were attracted to it because structurally it is the ancestor of the ice cream soda, where a non-alcoholic fruit flavored "pop" is substituted for the wine and vanilla ice cream takes the place of the wine flavored whipped cream. By means of this mutation (from fewer calories to more) the syllabub became a Temperance drink, and in terms of Mrs. Horace Mann's *Christianity in the Kitchen*, more biblically acceptable.

Whipped Syllabub

Take a lump of sugar and rub it on the outside of a lemon until coloured, then put it into a pint of cream and sweeten to taste; squeeze in the juice of a lemon, and add a glass of Sherry or Madeira, mill to a froth and take off the froth as it rises, and drain it well in a sieve, then half fill a glass with red wine, and pile up the froth as high as possible.

1 pt. heavy whipping cream
½ cup superfine sugar
grated zest of 1 lemon

¼ cup lemon juice, strained
1 bottle claret, good quality
4 tblsp. Madeira

Kitchen technology and the quality of whipping cream has improved a bit since this recipe was written. Thus the procedure can be altered without harming the intended results. Beat the cream until stiff; then beat in the superfine sugar (do *not* use granulated or confectioner's), the lemon zest and lemon juice. When this is thoroughly blended, add the Madeira and beat smooth. If heavy whipping cream is used, there will be no need to drain it. Fill tall, lily-shaped wine glasses half full of claret; then pile up the cream into peaks. Garnish each glass with a fresh currant if available. Yield: Serves 10-12 persons.

NOTE: The "mill" referred to in the original recipe is a chocolate mill; these tedious wooden instruments served as whisks in colonial times.

« 13 »

STEWED SHAD À LA TOURAINE

[1845]

SOURCE: ELIZA ACTON.

Modern Cookery in All its Branches . . . *Philadelphia: Lea &*
Blanchard, 1847, page 76.

LIBRARY COMPANY OF PHILADELPHIA.

Recipe of Charles Schroeder, cook for the French Minister at Philadelphia until
1793, later proprietor of the Swan Hotel on the banks of the Schuylkill. Inserted
in the American edition by its editor Sarah J. Hale.

Charles Schroeder was actually a confectioner by profession. His talents far
exceeded the market in Philadelphia when the upheaval of the French Revolution
left him without an employer and a homeland. Like many of the French emigrés
who made Philadelphia their home, Schroeder adapted in order to survive. His
wife continued in the confectionery trade while Charles turned his energies to the
Swan, and lucky for Philadelphia he did. In the short span of his American career
(1793-1804), Schroeder established himself as a leading city restaurateur.[1] One of
the specialties of the Swan was shad, which Schroeder offered in a number of
inventive ways. This recipe was preserved by Anthony Morris of "Bolton" in Bucks
County, a Francophile who passed it along to Mrs. Hale through one of her friends.
We include it not only as a record of excellent shad cookery, for which Philadelphia
was justly famous, but also as an example of how an ostensibly early Victorian
cookbook can offer up nuggets of "lost" material on the 18th century. In other
words, it is not the date of publication that counts as much as the age of the
material included. This concept can be a very useful tool to the culinary historian.

Shad Touraine Fashion (Alose à la mode de Touraine)

Empty and wash the fish with care, but do not open it more than is
needful; fill it either with the forcemeat No. 1, or No. 2 of Chapter VI.,
and its own roe; then sew it up, or fasten it securely with very fine
skewers, wrap it in a thickly-buttered paper, and broil it gently for an
hour over a charcoal fire. Serve it with caper sauce, or with cayenne
vinegar and melted butter.

We are indebted for this receipt to a friend who has been long resident in
Touraine, at whose table the fish is constantly served, thus dressed, and is
considered excellent. It is likewise often gently stewed in the light white
wine of the country, and served covered with a rich bechamel.

---

[1]See William Woys Weaver, "When Shad Came In: Shad Cookery in Old Philadelphia,"
Petits Propos Culinaires 11 (June 1982), p. 7-19.

All well and good. The way Schroeder prepared it was the latter, with or without an oyster stuffing. We offer two alternative methods of treatment, but in either case you will need:

1 shad, 3-4 lbs., leaving the head
   and tail on
1 qt. dry light white wine

1 qt. water
Bechamel sauce (see below)

Clean the shad and then lay the fish on a fish slice (i.e., rack). Set this in a fish pan, and add the water and wine. Poach until tender. Serve the fish whole on a hot platter surrounded by cooked diced potatoes garnished with chopped chives and steamed asparagus. Decorate the eye of the fish with a small slice of stuffed olive or a piece of egg white with a pupil made from a truffle or black olive. Serve the sauce in a sauce boat or over the fish. This should be sufficient for six persons.

Bechamel Sauce

4 tblsp. butter
3 tblsp. flour
2 cups cold milk
small slice of onion

1 fresh bay leaf, bruised (or 1-2 dry)
¼ tsp. mace
¼-½ cup white mushroom stock (see next
   page)
salt and white pepper to taste

Fry the flour and butter to make a blond roux. Add milk, onion, bay leaf, and mace. Cook and whisk until it thickens. Strain. Thin with white mushroom stock and season.

White Mushroom Stock
Recipe of James Parkinson

¼ cup water or milk
2 oz. butter
juice of ½ lemon, or 2-3 tblsp.
   lime juice

2 lb. mushrooms, washed and stemmed
1 fresh bay leaf, bruised (or 1-2 dry)
1 small clove garlic, cut in half

Heat the water, lemon juice, and butter until the butter melts. Add the fresh, bruised bay leaf and garlic. Then add the mushrooms. Cover closely, and simmer approximately 15 minutes, or until the mushrooms change color and throw their liquid. Strain off the liquid and use as directed. Yield: 1½ cups stock.

NOTE: The mushrooms may be served hot with the fish. Mushroom stock is not very much in fashion of late, but in shad cookery it was considered a necessity. Part of the difficulty is that many cooks use too much lemon, which makes it sour, and indeed, ½ lemon may be too much even in the recipe above.

The second method (we said there were two), is to serve the shad with shad roe sauce. For those directions, refer to recipe 30.

LEMON ICE CREAM
[1851]

SOURCE: Germantown Telegraph, *Philadelphia, August 20, 1851.*

We know from city newspaper advertisements that the most popular flavors of ice cream in the 1840s and 1850s were vanilla, lemon, strawberry, and pineapple. Some ice cream saloons, such as Parkinson's, offered a much larger selection but at luxury prices. Smaller establishments like that of William Hart on North 5th Street made water ices, sorbets, and such additional ice cream flavors as almond, tea, or chocolate on special order.[1] In an age before pasteurized cream and preservatives, even frozen ice creams did not keep indefinitely, thus arrangements such as Hart's were designed to keep quality up and spoilage down.

Eber Seamen's invention of the commercial ice cream machine in 1848 soon led to household models and a large shift in the kinds of ice creams the saloons could offer to the public. Before the coming of the crank-turned devices, Philadelphia style ice cream was made largely by freezing, beating, and refreezing flavored sweetened whipped cream. There is nothing wrong with frozen whipped cream, as long as we remember that it was a luxury food served in very small portions — "dainty" portions was the old term.

A common method for making lemon ice cream was to freeze it in a mold and serve up the sculpture at the last minute, as in the recipe we have chosen here. James Parkinson, Philadelphia's ice cream "king," made a harp of ice cream surmounted by an ice cream nightingale (realistically colored) for the Swedish soprano Jenny Lind, a culinary *tour de force* incidentally, which deeply impressed her.[2] We shall not suggest that you attempt a harp or even one of the strings, because most household cooks in the 1850s rarely possessed the necessary patience or equipment. But many did own tin or copper melon molds of the sort pictured here, and the quantity given in our recipe will fill a one quart mold comfortably. Lacking that, use a tin or copper pudding mold. Whatever you use, clean it thoroughly first and be certain it has a tight-fitting lid. If your container is made of copper, check that it is well tinned inside and out.

---

[1] *[Philadelphia] Sunday Dispatch,* May 6, 1849.
[2] *[Philadelphia] M'Makin's Model American Saturday Courier,* October 26, 1850.

Lemon Ice Cream

From two quarts of cream take one pint, into which stir one pound of powdered sugar, and the juice and grated rind of four lemons. Then beat the above mixture into the remaining three pints of cream. Strain and freeze. Milk and arrowroot may be substituted for cream, when that article cannot be procured.

Although this recipe is very clear, it would be useful to keep in mind that the cream used then is equivalent to our heavy cream today and that the "powdered sugar" is not confectioner's sugar but *superfine* sugar, which dissolves quickly. Granulated sugar must be reduced to a syrup before it can be used, but syrup will destroy the proportions and texture of this ice. The cream must be beaten until stiff before the various ingredients are folded together. It is not necessary to strain the batter, but it is necessary to avoid using a standard crank-turned or electronic maker; over beating will deflate it.

15

QUARTERLY MEETING PIE

[1851]

SOURCE: ELIZABETH E. LEA.

Domestic Cookery. *Baltimore: Cushing & Bailey, 1851,*
page 89.

ROUGHWOOD COLLECTION.

Copy of Susan W. Biddle (1823-1892) of Philadelphia, a gift from her father,
Clement Biddle, Jr., who was a sugar refiner in Philadelphia and co-partner in the
firm Biddle and Lea.

Recipe of Elizabeth Ellicott Lea (1793-1858) of Sandy Spring, Maryland.
Elizabeth Lea was a Quaker; daughter of George Ellicott, founder of Ellicott
Mills, Maryland; and wife of Thomas Lea, a member of a prominent Delaware
milling family.[1]

"Quarterly Meeting Pie" was a term used among Philadelphia Quakers for baked
potato pudding. It was a popular dessert dish served at Quarterly Meeting dinners,
when Quakers converged to attend to church business. Elizabeth Lea called it by
its more standard name: "Potato Pudding."

Potato Pudding

Take a pound and a half of well mashed potatoes; while they are warm
put in three-quarters of a pound of butter; beat six eggs with three-
quarters of a pound of sugar, rolled fine, mix all well together, and put in
a glass of brandy; season with nutmeg, mace or essence of lemon, and
bake in paste.

With the permission of Carl G. Sontheimer, President of the
Cuisinart Cooking Club, we reproduce below a modern
adaptation of Elizabeth Lea's recipe, which appeared in *The*
Pleasures of Cooking.[2] It is intended to illustrate how an old,
traditional recipe may be interpreted through modern
technology without sacrificing the integrity of the original.

[1]For an account of Elizabeth Lea's life and cookbook, refer to
William Woys Weaver, ed., *A Quaker Woman's Cookbook: The*
Domestic Cookery of Elizabeth Ellicott Lea (Philadelphia:
University of Pennsylvania Press, 1982).
[2]William Woys Weaver, "Choice Recipes from Old Philadelphia,"
The Pleasures of Cooking, VIII:3 (Nov./Dec. 1985), p. 8.

2 medium all-purpose potatoes (14 oz. total), peeled and quartered
1½ sticks unsalted butter (6 oz.), at room temperature, cut into 12 pieces
⅔ cup sugar (5 oz.)
3 tblsp. cognac
1 tsp. freshly ground nutmeg
½ tsp. ground mace
3 large eggs, separated
Short pastry (use your favorite pie crust)

To make the filling, cook the potatoes in boiling water to cover until tender, about 20 minutes. Drain. Process the potatoes while still warm with the medium shredding disc of a food processor. Leave the potatoes in the work bowl and insert the metal blade. Add the remaining ingredients except the egg whites and process until smooth, about 10 seconds, scraping down the work bowl as necessary.

Preheat the oven to 375°F.

Beat the egg whites until stiff but not dry, and fold in the potato mixture. Spread the filling in the prepared pastry crust, and bake in the center of the preheated oven for 10 minutes. Lower the heat to 325°F, and bake until the center of the pie is firm and the top is golden brown, about 35 minutes more.

Serve at room temperature. Makes 8 servings.

15. *Elizabeth E. Lea*

16

CHERRY TARTLETS

[1855]

SOURCE: HANNAH BOUVIER PETERSON.

The National Cook Book. *Philadelphia: Child & Peterson, 1855, page 137.*

ROUGHWOOD COLLECTION.

Recipe: As depicted in William E. Winner's 1856 painting "The Pie Man at the Corner of 5th and Chestnut Streets," in the collection of the Historical Society of Pennsylvania.

We were challenged to reproduce the various pastries shown on the tray in Winner's painting (on page 49), a task that may seem somewhat formidable to the layman. Actually, close inspection of the painting with a magnifying glass and a view expanded by newspaper descriptions of street foods in the 1850s made this task a relatively easy one. The painting probably records an actual vendor at the time. The season appears to be late June or early July, when cherries were at their peak. The small cakes on the back of the tray are the common "Dutch cakes" of commerce, baked in small oblong molds and iced—descriptive recipes for them abound. They were sold to children for six cents. On the front of the tray are cherry tartlets.

The only difficulty with our challenge was that we could not uncover a recipe for cherry tartlets actually used by a street vendor. But that would not affect the authenticity of the experiment, since vendors like this one generally sold on consignment for one or more pastry shops rather than undertaking the baking themselves. Thus, we chose a contemporary recipe that incorporates all the common technical features of typical pastry shop goods.

Hannah Peterson's recipe was intended for pie, not tartlets, thus it was necessary to look at a number of other cookbooks from the 1850s to see how the matter was handled. From this, we were able to determine that it was common practice to leave the cherry pits in the cherries, both to enhance the flavor (much of the flavor is in the pits) and to hold the shape of the fruit. Street urchins like those in the painting simply spit the pits out; in genteel circles, there was a "proper" ritual for removing the pits from the lips and depositing them with a fork at the side of one's plate. It has been said that in Philadelphia the litmus test for good breeding was not so much one's ability to make a salad (see recipe 19) but the way one handled those pits. In any case, while we much prefer the pits removed, here is how to reconstruct the tartlets in an "archeologically correct" manner.

Cherry Pie

Stew your cherries with sugar, in the proportion of a pound of cherries to half a pound of sugar, and stir in a little flour to thicken the syrup. Make a paste, as rich as you like, line your pie plates, fill with the fruit, and cover with a lid of the paste.

2 lb. sweet cherries, *unpitted*	⅓ cup red currant jelly
⅔ cup granulated sugar	2 tblsp. raw cherry juice or water
	2 tblsp. flour

Wash the fruit and remove the stems. Dissolve the jelly and sugar in the water or raw cherry juice. Bring this to a hard boil, and continue to boil until it forms a syrup. Add 1 pound of fruit, stir, cover, and simmer 10 minutes. Strain out the fruit and set aside to cool. Reheat the syrup, and repeat the process with the remaining 1 pound of cherries.

Line 14-16 tartlet pans (tin patty pans) with short pie crust. The pans should measure approximately 3½ inches in diameter and 1 inch deep. Prick the bottoms, crimp the edges, and bake at 350°F for roughly 15-20 minutes, or until crisp. Remove the tartlet shells from the pans, and cool on racks.

Reduce the syrup in which the cherries were stewed with two tablespoons of flour and cook until thick, or add ⅔ cup of currant jelly and reduce to a glaze. Fit the cherries into tartlet shells and add a few tablespoons of syrup or glaze to each. Let this cool; then pipe a decorative border of meringue around the outside edge of each tartlet. Make the meringue in the following manner:

2 egg whites
2 tblsp. superfine sugar
1 tblsp. Maraschino de Zara

Beat the whites until stiff; then fold in the sugar and liqueur. After piping the meringue on the tartlets, brown it a bit in the oven (5 minutes at 350°F) or with a very hot salamander (the old method).

16. William E. Winner, *"The Pie Man at the Corner of 5th and Chestnut Streets,"*
1856.

PEPPER HASH

[1855]

SOURCE: Housekeepers' Almanac and Family Receipt Book.
Philadelphia: King and Baird, 1855, page 30.

ROUGHWOOD COLLECTION.

When Victorian Americans thought of pepper hash, they immediately thought of Philadelphia much in the same way that a similar connection is made with hoagies today. Like the hoagie, pepper hash had a working class appeal: it was an inevitable condiment in oyster and fish houses all across the city. Fish cooks paired it up with fried oysters, soft-shell crabs, cod fish balls, shad fritters, and grilled catfish. As a condiment, it was not meant to be sweet but to take the place of the lemon juice one normally squeezed over fries.

Today, pepper hash is usually made with too much sugar and therefore does not marry as well with fish. The recipe we have chosen here is similar to the famous pepper hash served at Mrs. Watkins's Catfish and Coffee House that for many years stood by the Falls of the Schuylkill.[1] Her catfish suppers were once a city institution, a tradition that today has all but disappeared.

Pepper Hash

1 dozen large green peppers, 1 small head of cabbage, 3 cents worth each of mustard seed, cloves, and allspice, *all whole*, a teaspoonful *ground* cloves and allspice. Salt to your taste.

Chop the peppers and cabbages, mix thoroughly with the spices, put all in a jar, and cover with boiling vinegar.

6 medium green peppers
1 head of cabbage (approx. 3 lbs.)
3 tblsp. mustard seed
1 tsp. whole clove

1 tsp. whole allspice
1 qt. white vinegar + 1 cup
½ cup sugar or more to taste
4 tblsp. pickling salt
optional: 4 cloves garlic, sliced in half

---

[1] *[Philadelphia] Sunday Dispatch*, July 2, 1848

HOUSEKEEPERS' ALMANAC

FOR THE YEAR **18** AND FAMILY **55**

RECEIPT BOOK.

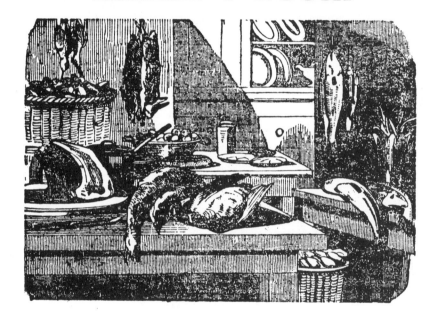

PHILADELPHIA:

PUBLISHED BY KING & BAIRD,

No. 9 SANSOM STREET

17. Roughwood Collection

Shred the cabbage paper thin and scatter salt over it. Stand in a colander and drain overnight. At the same time, make a small bag with clean linen or cheesecloth and fill it with the mustard, clove, and allspice. Bring the vinegar to a hard boil, add the bag and boil 5 minutes. Then add the garlic (optional). Cover and let stand overnight.

In the morning, remove the bag and the garlic from the vinegar and rinse the cabbage twice.

Mince or chop the peppers after removing the veins and seeds and mix with the cabbage. Bring the sugar and vinegar to a boil, and pour over the cabbage mixture. Stew this in a preserving kettle for 10 minutes; then pack in hot sterilized jars. Give the jars a 10-minute water bath, or, let the pepper hash cool and store in a glass container in the refrigerator until needed. It should keep two to three weeks under refrigeration. Yield: approximately 4 pints.

NOTE: The original recipe calls for 12 peppers, but as peppers were small in the 1850s, an adjustment must be made in the ratio of roughly two to one. Furthermore, the·recipe allows for the mustard seed to be put in with the chopped pepper *if so desired* (many people did not like mustard seed in the hash.) We may also suggest that ½ cup additional sugar may be added if the hash seems too sharp. We have suggested garlic in our tested recipe because Mrs. Watkins used garlic in hers.

« 18 »

SCRAPPLE

[1856]

SOURCE: ELIZABETH NICHOLSON.

What I Know; or Hints on the Daily Duties of a

Housekeeper. *Philadelphia: Willis P. Hazard, 1856, page 30.*

HISTORICAL SOCIETY OF PENNSYLVANIA.

Scrapple is a medieval dish, a survival from a time when pot puddings were part of daily fare. Court cooks put pot puddings inside pastry crusts instead of pouring them into molds as we do with scrapple. By degrees, this baked form evolved into the terrines and pâtés of present haute cuisine. Scrapple did not undergo that sort of evolution, although it is in every sense a primitive form of pâté. In Westphalia and northeastern Holland—the region from which Philadelphia scrapple originates —*Pannas*, as it is called there, is thickened with blood and buckwheat flour. In Philadelphia, animal blood had a commercial use in the processing of sugar and thus could be sold profitably. This is perhaps one reason why blood disappeared relatively early from our scrapple recipes, and the buckwheat was cut in half with cornmeal, allowing even less ground meat per pound of scrapple than in its European counterpart. In this sense, scrapple evolved, not into haute cuisine, but into an American original, or at least, into something distinctly different from its north German ancestors.

Scrapple was a dish eaten in connection with butchering day festivities; it was therefore a cold weather dish made from October to March. Commercial scrapple is now available all year round, but originally, it was never considered a hot weather dish, mainly because it could not be stored for any length of time. Making scrapple at home today is not economical; to be economical, scrapple must be made on a relatively large scale. That was no problem in the days when many households kept a few pigs. Elizabeth Nicholson's recipe presumes that her readers have their own pigs to butcher. Her scrapple recipe is typical and probably dates from the 18th century.

HASLET

Scrapple

Take a pig's haslet and as much offal lean and fat pork as you wish, to make scrapple; boil them well together in a small quantity of water until they are tender; chop them fine, after taking them out of the liquor; season, as sausage: then skim off the fat that has arisen where the meat was boiled, to make all soft, throw away the rest of the water, and put this altogether in the pot; thickening it with ½ buckwheat and ½ Indian. Let it boil up, then pour out in pans to cool. Slice and fry it in sausage-fat, after the sausage is done.

The seasonings that Nicholson uses in her sausages are salt, pepper, cloves, and sage. We have included them in the following recipe for a small batch of scrapple.

3 lb. fatty pork (no bones or gristle)	2 tsp. salt
3 qt. water	1½ tsp. fresh ground pepper (or more to taste)
1½ cups buckwheat flour	
1½ cups parched cornmeal or yellow cornmeal	1½ tblsp. ground sage (or more to taste)
	¼ tsp. ground cloves

Simmer the meat in the water 3½ to 4 hours, or until tender. Strain the broth and reduce it to two quarts. Grind the meat and any fat with it (half may be ground coarse, half fine). Weigh out 2 lbs. ground meat, stir this into the broth. Add the cornmeal, buckwheat, salt, pepper, sage, and cloves, and boil until thick. Stir often to keep the mixture smooth. Additional water may be added if it thickens too quickly, but when it is ready for the molds, the scrapple should have the consistency of mashed potatoes. Grease six 6-inch bread pans and pour the batter into it. Let this stand until cool, then refrigerate over night. In the morning, turn the scrapple out, slice and fry what is wanted, or slice and freeze.

To fry scrapple, heat a heavy iron skillet or frying pan over a high flame, then turn back the heat to low and lay the slices of scrapple in the pan. Let it fry very slowly until crisp and golden brown; then turn it over and fry the other side.

NOTE: It was customary to pour melted pork fat over the scrapple to seal it before cooling. This small layer of fat, which appears as a white line on the bottom of each slice, was used to grease the pan for frying.

19

SALAD DRESSING
[1868]

SOURCE: Germantown Telegraph, *Philadelphia, March 18, 1868*.

LIBRARY COMPANY OF PHILADELPHIA.

It was formerly the custom in Philadelphia for the husband to market for the salad and with no small flourishing put it all together at table. Gentlemen were judged by their salads, and not the least important, by the whole manner of blending the dressing. Elizabeth Pennell, the great cookbook collector, recalled this ritual in *Our Philadelphia* with obvious nostalgia.[1]

She would have delighted in the battle of letters, the salvos of recipes, and other culinary crossfire that erupted in the *Germantown Telegraph* in the late 1860s over the proper mode for dressing lettuce. We thought that the following poem was indeed the last blast, but it wasn't. It only precipitated another round of culinary discharge in prosaic and poetic form, and so the issue tossed, from Germantown into the salad bowl and back. One further note: the Sidney Smith mentioned in the poem was the author of several bestselling books, among them *Salad for the Solitary* and *Salad for the Social*. One of his poems contained a recipe for salad dressing that gained widespread popularity in the press. It was submitted to the *Germantown Telegraph* by a feminine reader as part of the recipe exchange, to which the following was a response.

Salad Dressing

> Your good lady Salad-maker forgot to say
> That Sidney Smith composed her famous lay.
> He praises anchovy and onion; they're enough
> To frighten every dainty palate from the stuff.
> If you *must* have potato—why? I cannot see,
> Let it be only *one*, and let it mealy be.
> I think none needed, for the yolks of boiled eggs
> Keep up the dressing's body well upon it legs.
> I made the blind Reverend's mixture, and I found
> It stiff and dry—not heavenly, too much of ground;
> Two hard boiled yolks from barn-door fowls you'll need;
> Keep those from far off Brahma and Houdan to breed;
> Of Durham mustard a full teaspoon grant;

---

[1] Elizabeth and Joseph Pennell, *Our Philadelphia* (Philadelphia: J.B. Lippincott, 1914), p. 433-434.

The same of salt and sugar fine you'll want;
A dash of capsicum excites the whole,
And keeps the Durham under good control;
Fill twice the spoon with vinegar quite clear;
Rub well the solids till no lumps appear.

Now pour the oil of gladness—let it be
The sweetest, purest from the olive tree;
Stint not your spending—get the finest, best;
Without it, time is idly spent with all the rest;
Rub in three tablespoonsful at discretion,
'Tis hard to get too much—it's my impression.

Come forth crisp lettuce! Hot-bed! quick reveal;
Oh! Cut it with knife silvered—not with steel
Pour on the soft persuader—stir by slow degrees;
Eat as a course, alone—add only biscuit hard and cheese.

Montgomery County, Pa.

To untangle the puzzle, here are the ingredients you will need:

yolks of 2 hard boiled eggs
1 tsp. mustard
1 tsp. salt
1 tsp. superfine sugar

dash of pepper
2 tblsp. vinegar
3 tblsp. olive oil

Work all the ingredients except the olive oil to a smooth paste. Add the oil, pour the dressing onto the salad, toss and serve.

20

FRENCH ROLLS

⟦ 1870 ⟧

SOURCE: FRANCES A. KEMBLE.

The Manuscript Receipt Book and Household Treasury.

Philadelphia: Claxton, Remsen & Haffelfinger,

c. 1870, page 144.

ROUGHWOOD COLLECTION.

This is a blank cookbook divided into chapters, which are then filled in with manuscript recipes. Compiled at "Butler Place" near Chestnut Hill.

Frances Anne Kemble (1809-1893) did not make her mark in the arena of cookery. Her *American Journal* (1835), her scandalous divorce from Pierce Butler, her *Journal of a Residence on A Georgian Plantation* (1863), and of course her fame as an actress placed her in the realm of international celebrity.[1] This then, is a celebrity recipe.

We have taken it directly from Fanny Kemble's manuscript which she evidently compiled at Butler Place for her daughter Mrs. Owen Jones Wister. There is every reason to believe that Sarah Wister continued the manuscript and that her famous son, novelist Owen Wister, ate many of the very same dishes prepared from recipes in this book.

We chose the French roll recipe because French rolls (what many people call "pocket-book rolls" today) were once symbols of status at table. They were the manchet breads of the 17th century gentry and the small wheaten breads of the 18th century well-to-do. This particular recipe was quite popular in 19th century America. In fact, it appeared in Mrs. Chadwick's *Home Cookery* (Boston, 1852), and doubtless found its way into other printed cookbooks as well.

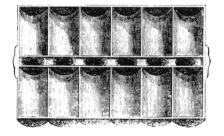

---

[1]For a history of her career, see Fanny Kemble Wister, *Fanny: The American Kemble* (Tallahassee: South Pass Press, 1972).

The trick to making French rolls the proper way—as the Victorians made them—is to use a French roll pan and a French roll rolling pin. The pan (page 57) helps maintain the shape during baking. The rolling pin enables the cook to roll out each ball of dough and fold it over to the correct shape. The rolling pin is nothing more than a miniature version of the large ones, about six inches long and roughly the size of a broom handle in diameter. Antique dealers sell them as "rolling pins for little girls," but this is no place to digress on popular mythologies. The important thing is the attractive shape, the finish of the crust, and the texture of the bread. In a nation like ours, where good bread is a rare commodity, the extra effort put into a recipe like this one will produce applause at table.

For 16 rolls:

2 tblsp. butter	¾ cup milk
1 lb. flour, double sifted (approx. 3½ cups)	¼ oz. pkg. yeast dissolved in ¼ cup lukewarm milk
1 egg	1 tsp. salt

Rub the butter into the flour by working it through a sieve. Beat the egg to a froth; add the milk and the proofed yeast. Beat thoroughly; then make a hole in the center of the flour, and pour the liquid in it. Using a large wooden or plastic fork, work this up into a soft dough. Cover and let rise until double in bulk. Knock down and mold out into 16 2-oz. balls of dough. Weighing them will insure uniform size. Take the small rolling pin and roll each ball so that it is somewhat flat on top and beginning to take on an oblong shape. Brush this surface with melted butter, and then fold it over. Repeat this with each ball of dough. Set the rolls in a greased French roll pan (failing that, use a baguette pan) and let them rise one hour. Bake in an oven preheated to 425° F for 10-12 minutes. Brush with cold water as soon as they are done. Cool on racks.

French Rolls

Rub 1 oz butter into a lb. of flour, mix an egg well beaten a little yeast, and as much milk as will make dough of a moderate stiffness, beat it well, beat it well, but do not knead it, let it rise — To be baked in tin pans

21

DREDGING MIXTURE FOR ROAST MUTTON
[1871]

SOURCE: ESTHER JACOBS LEVY.

Jewish Cookery Book, on Principles of Economy.

Philadelphia: W.S. Turner, 1871, page 41.

LIBRARY COMPANY OF PHILADELPHIA.

Esther Levy's dredging mixture is very much in the tradition of the spice powders and other similar condiments that were once popular fixtures in the old Philadelphia kitchen.[1] Her recipe appears so simple that it is deceiving. Its secret is in the doing. And once done, we believe that it will be done many times again, if for no other reason than that it is one easy and sensible way to eliminate sauces, and therefore reduce calories.

Roast Mutton (A Shoulder)

Take some flour, ginger, and salt, and rub it over the mutton. Bake it with some sage, onions, and split potatoes, in a good oven. Eat it with either boiled onions, currant or jelly sauce.

The following is sufficient for 2 lb. of mutton or lamb.

2 tblsp. flour
1 tsp. powdered ginger

¼ tsp. salt
¼ cup fresh chopped sage

Lasteyrie del.

---

[1]For example, see William Woys Weaver, "Schinckel's Spice Powder," *Petits Propos Culinaires 10* (London, 1982), p. 39-40.

Mix the flour, ginger and salt. Rub this over the meat as directed in the recipe. Place the onions and split potatoes around the roast, and scatter half of the sage over them. When the roast is done, scatter the remaining sage over the meat and serve.

מלאכת הבישול בדרך נכון וכפי מצות דתנו הקדושה

A COOKERY BOOK PROPERLY EXPLAINED, AND
IN ACCORDANCE WITH THE RULES OF THE JEWISH RELIGION.

JEWISH

COOKERY BOOK,

ON

PRINCIPLES OF ECONOMY,

ADAPTED FOR

JEWISH HOUSEKEEPERS,

WITH THE ADDITION OF MANY USEFUL MEDICINAL RECIPES,

AND

Other Valuable Information,

RELATIVE TO HOUSEKEEPING AND DOMESTIC MANAGEMENT.

By MRS. ESTHER LEVY,

(Neé Esther Jacobs.)

PHILADELPHIA:

W. S. TURNER, No. 808 CHESTNUT STREET.

1871.

21. First Jewish cookbook printed in America.

22

FISH HOUSE PUNCH

⟦ 1873 ⟧

SOURCE: DR. WILLIAM CAMAC. Governor of the State in Schuylkill.
Fish House Punch. *MS*. *[Philadelphia, ca. 1873].*

HISTORICAL SOCIETY OF PENNSYLVANIA.

The State in Schuylkill, known as "The Fish House," is the oldest private club in the United States. Founded in 1732 as a fishing club, it has persisted to this day through all the vicissitudes of time, not to mention the burning of the clubhouse in 1980. Membership is limited to 30, which is a useful number to keep in mind when perusing the old recipes for Fish House Punch.

Many people have heard of Fish House Punch; few know its historical connection with the club; fewer yet have tasted the real article, since numerous ersatz recipes are now in circulation. Most of them are thoroughly undrinkable and do no service to the honor of the club that made this beverage famous.

Therefore, we have gone to the source, or at least to one of them. The recipe on the following page is the original manuscript from which we have adapted ours. We have changed nothing, except to adjust the proportions to what Dr. Camac referred to as a "moderate family tipple."

1 cup fresh lemon juice pressed from lemons with the rinds removed
1 cup cognac of the best quality (Salignac V.S. will do)

1 cup light rum
1¼ lb. superfine sugar (essential)
4½ cups spring water or bottled water (NEVER, NEVER use Philadelphia tap water)

Dissolve the sugar in two cups of spring water. Stir until clear. Strain the lemon juice and add it to the water; then add the cognac and rum. Add the rest of the water, using as much of the remaining 2½ cups, or as little, as taste demands. Less water is necessary if the punch is served over crushed ice; more if served over ice cubes.

When making large batches for punch bowls filled with ice, it was customary to hold out a pitcher of the strong solution before adding the last portion of water so that the punch could be reseasoned as the ice melted, this to keep it up to strength. There are several ways of making a large quantity successfully, but our family tipple yields about ½ gallon, and that is quite enough for a small gathering given the results of one or two cups. Had the Fish House served this to the British when they occupied Philadelphia, we have no doubt the Revolution would have come to a crashing close long before Yorktown.

Fish House Punch.

from D. W. Camac
Governor of the
State in Schuylkill

One quart of Lemon Juice
One quart of Brandy.
Two quarts of Rum.
Five pounds of Sugar,
Nine pounds of Water and ice, i.e. $4\frac{1}{2}$ quarts.

Method: Dissolve the sugar in one pint of water.
Strain the lemon juice and add it to the dissolved
sugar.
(To make a perfect punch the rind of the lemon should be taken off
to prevent the oil getting into the punch)

Then add the Rum and Brandy, with 2 quarts of
water.   Let this mixture be made very
thorough by frequent stirring.

(There remains $2\frac{1}{4}$ quarts of water and ice or about 5 lbs. of ice.)

Remove a portion of this mixture into a pitcher
with which to strengthen and replenish later.
Put about 3 lbs. of ice in the bowl and in $\frac{3}{4}$
of an hour the punch is ready.
When the punch is getting low or has weakened
by the dissolved ice, add the reserve mixture

from the pitcher with the remaining two lbs.
of ice.

This makes about $2\frac{1}{4}$ gallons of punch. for a moderate
family tipple. one-fourth the quantity may be enough.

23

CARAMEL ICE CREAM
[1874]

SOURCE: The Confectioners' Journal. *Philadelphia, Dec. 1874,*
I:1, page 5.

Recipe of James W. Parkinson, Philadelphia confectioner.

The cream caramels of Henrion and Chauveau of Philadelphia were world famous in the 19th century. The firm sold as many of its confections in Vienna and Paris as it did in New York or Philadelphia. James Parkinson described their candies as "beyond imitation," and doubtless he was right, since no manner of recipe sleuthing can ever recapture the genius touch of truly great cooks.[1] But Parkinson did conjure up the spirit of the Henrion and Chauveau cream caramels in a little invention of his own that comes to us in the form of an ice cream. It is meant to suggest the texture and flavor of cream caramel. Whether or not it succeeds in this respect, it is perhaps the most luxurious, incomparably good soft ice cream this side of Paradise. The semi-frozen chemical froth sold as soft ice cream along the road today is not even worthy of comparison.

1½ pts. heavy cream (3 cups)	4 oz. granulated sugar
1 stick cinnamon, coarsely broken into small pieces	10 egg yolks
zest of 1 lemon	4 tblsp. Orange Curaçoa
12 oz. superfine sugar	1 cup water

Take 4 oz. granulated sugar and add to it 3 tblsp. water and 1 tsp. lemon juice. Stir this together, then bring to a boil in a saucepan over a high heat. Do not stir the syrup as it boils, but rather, watch it carefully. Let it turn dark brown, almost black. When it begins to smoke, it is ready.

Work quickly. Add the grated zest of 1 lemon and the cinnamon. Stir until the burnt syrup begins to foam. Then add one cup of water, taking care not to spatter yourself with hot sugar. Continue to stir until all the burnt sugar is dissolved. Then let the "tea" cool.

---

[1]See "Choice Caramels," *Confectioners' Journal,* (Oct. 1877), III:33, p. 17.

While the tea is cooling, cream the egg yolks with 12 oz. superfine sugar. Beat the heavy cream until it begins to stiffen, then fold it into the egg and sugar mixture. Beat again, then strain the tea and work it into the batter. Heat the batter over a moderate flame and stir until it thickens to a custard consistency. Cool. Add the Curaçoa and freeze.

NOTE: It is not necessary to freeze this in an ice cream maker. Any clean, tinned copper or stainless steel container with a lid will serve the purpose. Because of the high proportion of invert sugar in this ice cream, it does not freeze solid under normal freezing conditions.

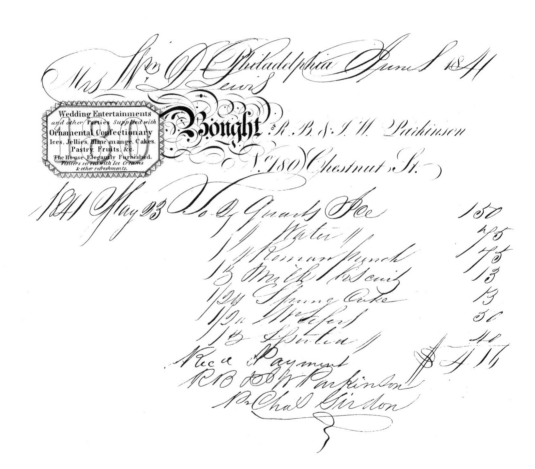

24

PHILADELPHIA FRIED OYSTERS

[1879]

SOURCE: The Confectioners' Journal. *Philadelphia, Dec. 1879, V:59, page 15.*

Recipe of L.F. Mazzetti, chef de cuisine of the West End Hotel, Philadelphia.

Before coming to the United States, Mazzetti served first as chef de cuisine of the Hotel de Ville in Milan, then at Dufour's in Paris. From there he went to Delmonico's in New York and later served as chef at the White House during the Grant Administration. After leaving the West End Hotel in 1879, Mazzetti joined the New York firm of H. Ughetta & Co., confectioners and pastry cooks. He was considered one of the most brilliant chefs working in Philadelphia during the 1870s.[1] The West End, where he was employed, was a center of culinary innovation during its short period of existence from 1877 to 1889. It was located at 1522 Chestnut Street and in 1889 was demolished to make way for another building.

It is important to remember that Mazzetti did not invent this recipe; it had been in circulation among professional chefs in the city at least since the 1820s and perhaps earlier. The name derives from the fact that it was in Philadelphia that the technique for deep frying oysters reached its perfection.[2] The recipe was considered a trade secret until James Parkinson published it in the *Confectioners' Journal*. The strategy of the recipe was to produce a fried oyster with a crisp, flaky, paper-thin crust and absolutely no hint of grease. We might add, the strategy works!

Philadelphia Fried Oysters

To have a dry and soft crust on oysters, and to make the so-called Philadelphia fried oysters, take the best and largest, fresh opened; sprinkle with salt and let them remain on a cullender an hour, in a cool place, to free them from superfluous water, which otherwise would escape as soon as they feel the heat, cooling your frying fat and making your crust moist and greasy. Spread them on cracker dust, turning them in it and allowing them to remain ten minutes; meantime, beat separately one egg to each dozen oysters, with as much of their juice [2 tblsp.] and a little

---

[1] *Confectioners' Journal*, (Jan. 1880), V:60, p. 15.
[2] William Woys Weaver, "Was There A Philadelphia Style?," *Proceedings: Current Research in Culinary History: Sources, Topics, and Materials*, Jillian Strang, et al., eds. (Hingham, Mass.: Culinary Historians of Boston, 1986), p. 85-94.

pepper. Have ready a stale loaf of bread, grate in the same way as cheese; also see that the lard you fry them in be not only *boiling* hot, but *frying* hot; that is, has stopped bubbling and boiling and come to stand, giving out smoke instead of steam. Have enough of this lard in the pan to let the oysters float; dip them in the beaten eggs and juice, then in the grated bread, and, without squeezing, plunge them in the fat, a few at a time; take them up with a skimmer when they have obtained a dark brown color, which will take about a minute, if prepared as above.

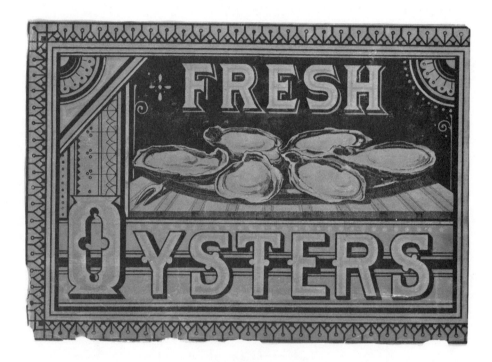

We cannot improve on these directions, except to list more explicitly the ingredients you will need:

12 large oysters	1 egg
salt	2 tblsp. oyster juice
breadcrumbs	cayenne pepper
cracker dust	Crisco or lard for deep frying

Now, proceed as Mazzetti directs. Make the usual preparations for a champagne breakfast, good linens, flower arrangements, etc., and allow one bottle of Dom Perignon for each dozen oysters. Lock the doors, disconnect the phone and invite absolutely no one until you are certain all the oysters are gone.

25

BLACKBERRY PUDDING

[1886]

SOURCE: SARAH TYSON RORER.

Philadelphia Cook Book: A Manual of Home Economies.

Philadelphia: Arnold & Co., 1886, page 390.

HISTORICAL SOCIETY OF PENNSYLVANIA.

Recipe of Sarah Tyson Rorer (1849-1937), as taught in the Philadelphia Cooking School.

We have chosen this recipe as a typical example of Mrs. Rorer's home economics cooking philosophies: the number of eggs has been reduced in favor of a chemical leavener (therein lies part of the economy), and the entire dish depends for its success on a readily available mass-produced product, in this case, a tin pudding mold.

By the late 1880s, American-made pudding molds had become relatively cheap, and Mrs. Rorer is known to have used them extensively in her product testimonials and public demonstrations. Since this recipe is clear enough in the original, we provide it without a modernized version.

Blackberry Pudding

1 pint of milk
3½ cups of flour
3 eggs
½ teaspoonful of salt

1 tablespoonful of melted
  butter
2 heaping teaspoonsful of
  baking-powder
1 pint blackberries

Beat the eggs, whites and yolks together, until light; then add the milk, then the flour, and beat until smooth; then add the butter melted, salt and baking-powder. Drain the blackberries [after washing them], dredge them with flour, stir them into the pudding, and turn into a greased pudding mold. Cover, stand in a pot of boiling water, and boil continuously for three hours. If the water evaporates in the pot, replenish with boiling water. Serve with Fairy Butter.

Fairy Butter or Nun's Butter

This recipe appears on page 438 of Mrs. Rorer's cookbook. It is not the same as the fairy butter of Hannah Glasse or other 18th century writers.

¼ cup of butter
1 cup of powdered sugar

1 teaspoonful of sherry
whites of two eggs

Beat the butter to a cream, add gradually the sugar, and beat until very light; add the whites, one at a time, and beat all until very light and frothy, then add gradually the sherry and beat again. Heap it on a small dish, sprinkle lightly with grated nutmeg, and stand away on the ice to harden.

26

PEPPERPOT SOUP
⟦ 1890 ⟧

source: LIZZIE MARTIN.

[Recipe Book]. *MS. [Philadelphia, ca. 1890], page 73.*

LIBRARY COMPANY OF PHILADELPHIA.

Pepperpot is an old term for a family of hot, spicy soups originating in the West Indies as cultural hybrids of Spanish and West African cooking traditions. Essentially, Philadelphia pepperpot is gumbo without the okra although the earliest surviving recipes (from the 1760s) contain not only okra, but also chopped sunflowers and other curious ingredients. In any case, the pepperpot soup we know today, made with tripe and potatoes, is only one member of this large and diverse family, and certainly the least exotic.

This brings us to the dilemma that faced us when time came to choose a pepperpot recipe for this cookbook. The modern palate is not prepared for habañero peppers, salt mackerel or large quantities of animal organs, shell fish, corn, pumpkin or mushrooms all tossed rather informally into one pot. The golden essences of history are simply not there. Thus we turn to Lizzie Martin, whose identity remains an enigma, but whose recipe for pepperpot comes with the recommendation that it is makeable, eatable, and authentic, if not also rich in tripe.

Pepper Pot M.P. Martin

Take 4 lbs of tripe, ½ plain ½ honeycomb, *well boiled* the day before, put into a pot with one half of a large shin bone, a small red pepper, a few onions, 4 small potatoes cut up, and small dumplings, if wished—thyme, salt. Thicken, or not, as preferred—Let it boil slowly from breakfast until dinner, cut the tripe & meat in small pieces.

As is often the case in folk cookery, even the explicit seems to take on opaque dimensions when we get down to specifics. This recipe is no exception. We would feel more comfortable to present it as follows:

2 lb. plain tripe
2 lb. honeycomb tripe
½ shin bone (or 1½ lb. meaty stewing bone), yielding roughly 1½ cups chopped meat
1 small pod of cayenne pepper
3 onions (10-12 oz.), sliced

1½ lb. potatoes
1½ to 2 cups small dumplings (see page 70)
1 to 2 tsp. dry thyme
1 tblsp. salt or more to taste
6 quarts water

Cook the beef shin or bones, onions, and the pod of pepper, in the water for three hours. Strain and pick the meat from the bone. Set the meat aside until the tripe is ready, or, if the tripe has been cooked previously, then add the tripe and meat to the broth and simmer 35 minutes. Add the potato, thyme, and dumplings and continue cooking until the potatoes are done. Adjust seasoning and serve hot, hot, hot!

NOTE: It saves trouble to cook the tripe the day before, in which case, *do not boil* it as boiling toughens it. The best procedure is to bring a kettle of well-salted water to a hard boil, then lower the heat and add the tripe. *Poach* the tripe steadily until it is tender. By poaching we mean that the water should barely tremble.

Since the recipe calls for small dumplings, we append the following from Sara T. Paul, *Cookery from Experience* (Philadelphia, 1875), p. 18.

Dumplings for Pepper Pot

Rub into a pint of prepared flour an even tablespoon of good lard, add a saltspoonful of salt, mix into a rather soft dough with cold water, flour your paste-board, and roll out about a quarter of an inch in thickness, cut in long strips half an inch wide, and these into squares, dusting them with flour as you proceed to prevent their sticking together, drop them in the boiling soup and cook them ten minutes.

2 cups flour
1 tblsp. lard or Crisco

¼ tsp. salt
⅔ cup cold water

Follow the directions given above.

27

AUGUSTINE'S CHICKEN CROQUETTES
⟦ 1890 ⟧

SOURCE: LIZZIE MARTIN.

[Recipe Book]. *MS*. *[Philadelphia, ca. 1890], page 73.*

LIBRARY COMPANY OF PHILADELPHIA.

Recipe of Peter Augustine, Philadelphia caterer.

"The chicken croquette is the secret of Augustine—that of his sons, now that the original is dead—and it would be easier to obtain an advance copy of the President's Message than Augustine's croquette receipt."[1]

Augustine, you ask? Augustine. In the 19th century Augustine was enough to conjure up the most perfectly catered parties in the nation. Boston, New York, Philadelphia, Baltimore, Washington, that was Augustine territory—who else could afford him?

Peter Augustine was black. He came to Philadelphia from the West Indies, learned the catering trade from Robert Bogle, and then established himself in business in 1816.[2] Elizabeth Pennell likened him to a Vatel, Careme, and Gouffé in one persona.[3] She would know—she tasted his cooking; but we will leave history to be the judge of that. More important, Augustine virtually created a catering empire at a time when opportunities for blacks were extremely limited. The Augustines themselves became wealthy, yet they also created employment opportunities for other blacks, and by training young talent over several generations, the Philadelphia catering industry became basically a black industry and a highly successful one. The days of the white gloves are behind us, but Augustine's legacy remains, if not in the legends about his terrapin and broiled oysters, then at least in visions of his chicken croquettes.

Concerning Augustine's croquettes, Colonel Forney underestimated the creativity of the food historian and the inherent rewards of serendipity. To wit: a manuscript cookbook of no apparent interest came to light in the collection of the Library

---

[1]Col. John W. Forney, "Terrapin," *The Epicure* (New York: H.K. & F.B. Thurber & Co., 1879), p. 32.

[2]W.E.B. DuBois, *The Philadelphia Negro: A Social Study* (New York: Schocken Books, 1967), p. 34

[3]Elizabeth and Joseph Pennell, *Our Philadelphia* (Philadelphia/London: J.B. Lippincott Co., 1914), p. 438-440.

Company. The compiler, Lizzie Martin, remains an unknown entity among the multitudes of Philadelphia Lizzie Martins living in the 1890s. But this Lizzie had taste and a nose for culinary gold. After analyzing her collection, we realized that page after page, it recorded some of the rarest Philadelphia recipes and some of the best. On the same page with her recipe for pepperpot (see recipe 26), we spotted Augustine's croquettes. Now we offer you the recipe that Delmonicos sighed for and everyone thought the Augustines took to their graves.

Croquettes Augustine's Recipe

Put into a saucepan 1½ pts. of milk or cream, when hot stir into it, ¼ lb. of butter and 2 tablespoonfuls of flour, rubbed together and well mixed with some of the milk, ¼ of an onion chopped fine, boil until it thickens, then stir in the chicken, which has been chopped very fine, and well seasoned with salt, cayenne, and mace—mix well—cool the mixture, form into shapes, roll in crumbs, and yolk of an egg, and fry. A chicken weighing 5½ lbs. will make 12 croquettes.

9-10 cups finely chopped chicken meat
    or 6 cups chopped meat plus 2 cups
    bread crumbs
3 cups milk or cream
4 oz. butter
2 tblsp. flour
4 oz. onion, minced
1½ tsp. salt
¼ tsp. cayenne pepper
1 tsp. mace
breadcrumbs
egg yolk

The directions are fairly clear, so we have not attempted to alter them. If the croquettes are formed by hand on a surface dusted with cracker crumbs, there is no need to dip them in egg and breadcrumbs before frying. This will yield approximately 32 two-ounce croquettes. Fry three at a time, or the boiling oil will cool too much and the croquettes will become greasy. A word of advice: Augustine's croquettes must be flaky-crisp on the outside and creamy within, or not at all.

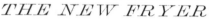

28

BARNARD CAKE

[1890]

SOURCE: FRANCES WILLEY.

The Model Cook Book. *Philadelphia: Empire Publishing Co.,*
1890, page 260.

ROUGHWOOD COLLECTION.

We have chosen this recipe for two reasons. First, Willey's cookbook is a useful
example of the inexpensively printed, mass-culture or "pulp" cookbooks that
Philadelphia printers found necessary to issue as competition from New York
became greater and greater after the U.S. Centennial. The book originally
appeared in 1884 in Troy, New York, one third the size of the Philadelphia edition.[1]
Doubtless, this is in itself evidence of what happened to a small, yet popular
regional cookbook when it fell into the hands of a large and aggressive publishing
house. It also speaks for the patchwork way in which cookbooks like Willey's grew
by accretion with little if any stylistic input by the author—stylistic in the sense of
uniform cooking style. As a result, her recipes are quite uneven in quality.
Fortunately, often buried in books of this sort are true culinary nuggets, which
brings us to the second reason for choosing Barnard cake.

Aside from the fact that it is a delightful and easy cake to make, Barnard cake might
rightly be called "Abolitionist Cake," since it was probably sold at benefits for
"passengers" on the Underground Railroad. We do not know how the recipe
reached Frances Willey, but we suspect that it came to her through the "Quaker
network." In any event, we do know the origin of the cake's name.

In the 19th century, the Barnards were a very well-known clan of Abolitionists
who centered their activities around Marlborough and Kennett Friends Meetings
in Chester County, Pennsylvania. Their web of Abolitionist activities ranged
nationwide, both through the Underground Railroad and through religious or
political contacts.[2] For example, Richard Meredith Barnard (1797-1854) of
Marlborough served as an Abolitionist in the State Legislature in 1837-1838 and
was a member of the Meeting for Sufferings of Philadelphia Yearly Meeting
(Hicksite) until his death.

---

[1] See Frances Willey, *The Model Cook Book* (Troy: E.H. List, 1884), no. 2156 in Eleanor &
Bob Brown, *Culinary Americana* (New York, 1961).
[2] Their activities are well-documented in R.C. Smedley, *History of the Underground
Railroad in Chester and Neighboring Counties of Pennsylvania* (Lancaster, Pa.: The
Journal, 1883).

Structurally, Barnard Cake is similar to 18th-century Queen Cake, and may, therefore be older than its popular name. Whatever its ultimate origin, for those who celebrate "Juneteenth," it makes a perfect and appropriate finale. No icing needed.

Barnard Cake

"One cup of butter, three cups of sugar, four and one-half cups of flour, four eggs, one cup of sour milk; the juice and a little of the rind of a lemon, and one teaspoon of saleratus."

1 cup butter
3 cups granulated sugar
4½ cups pastry flour
4 eggs

1 cup buttermilk
juice and grated zest of 1 lemon
1¼ tsp. baking soda

Cream the butter and sugar until light and fluffy. Beat the eggs to a froth and combine with the buttermilk. Beat the egg and butter mixture together, add the lemon; then sift together the flour and baking soda twice. Gradually sift and fold this into the batter. Grease two round 10-inch cake pans—preferably spring-form —and fill no more than ⅔ full. Bake in an oven preheated to 350°F for 45-50 minutes, or until the cakes test done. Cool on racks before removing from the pans.

NOTE: The flavor is better if all the rind of the lemon is used instead of "a little" as called for. This may be further augmented with 1 tsp. of lemon extract.

PLAIN SWEET CAKES.

29

BOBOTJE

[1890]

SOURCE: The Confectioners' Journal.

Philadelphia, Feb. 1890, XVI:181, page 71.

Bobotje is Afrikaans for "curried minced meat." Actually, the meat was also shaped in little molds, and thus may have contributed somewhat to the rise in popularity of the shaped meat loaf by the turn of this century. The precise date of introduction of bobotje to the United States may be difficult to pinpoint, but it is certainly true —as the *Confectioners' Journal* verifies—that it appeared in our professional literature far in advance of cookbooks. In any case, it became fashionable among Philadelphia fox hunting circles who were introduced to it from England, where it became stylish much earlier, having gone there directly from South Africa. To say the least, bobotje is one of those dishes that has traveled extensively and changed a bit in every port. Many later editions of Mrs. Beeton's *Household Management* contain recipes for it in the chapter on South African cookery, usually under its more common spelling "Bobotee." That is how it appears in *The Bethlehem Cook Book* (Bethlehem, Pa., 1900), *The Queen Esther Cook Book* (Vineland, N.J., 1906), and many other turn-of-the-century cookbooks from the Philadelphia region. The name may have appealed to old Philadelphia's penchant for the exotic, but in application, bobotje is a thoroughly practical means for adding interest to a hunt breakfast or supper. Its versatility recommends its revival.

Bobotjes

One large onion (chopped and fried), one tablespoonful of curry powder or paste, equal quantities of breadcrumbs (soaked in milk), and finely chopped chicken, beef or fish (cooked first), the juice of half a lemon, one egg, a little stock, pepper and salt; mix this over the fire for ten minutes, then pour it into buttered molds or cups. Stand these in a pan of hot water in a hot oven for fifteen minutes. Serve plain or with rice and a rich curry sauce. These bobotjes are considered indispensible at hunt breakfasts in England.

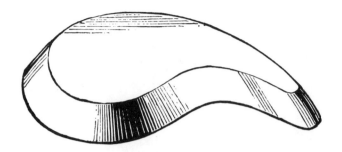

We have interpreted it thus:

2 cups finely grated cold boiled beef	3-4 tblsp. lemon juice
2 cups breadcrumbs	1 egg
12 oz. pureed onion (approx. 1½ cups)	2½ cups cold beef stock
3 tblsp. butter	¼ tsp. cayenne pepper
1 tblsp. + 1 tsp. curry powder	1 tsp. salt

Mix the meat, crumbs, curry powder, pepper and salt. Fry the onion until yellow, and add to the meat mixture. Add the lemon juice. Beat the egg to a froth with the beef stock, and work this into the dry ingredients (omitting the milk called for in the original recipe). Stir this over a low heat for 10 minutes, stirring constantly to keep it from scorching. Fill 18 greased tin forms (¾ inch deep, 2-3 inches in diameter, like those illustrated here). Set these in shallow water in baking trays and bake at 400°F for 15 minutes. Serve hot with curry sauce.

NOTE: Bobotje may be served cold without a sauce. In this case, lovage jelly is an excellent match.

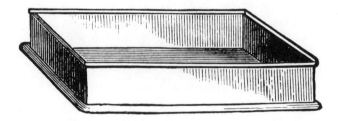

SHAD ROE SAUCE

⟦ 1894 ⟧

SOURCE: MINNIE PALMER.

The Woman's Exchange Cook Book, Or an Economical and Practical American Culinary Encyclopedia. *Chicago/ Philadelphia: Monarch Book Company, 1894, page 130.*

ROUGHWOOD COLLECTION.

We do not have Charles Schroeder's recipe for shad roe sauce, but as this recipe is rather typical in terms of structure, we do not hesitate to recommend it as a substitute.

Shad Roe Sauce

Wash 2 shad roes well in cold water. Put them in a small saucepan, add a teaspoonful of salt, cover with boiling water; put the lid on the saucepan, and simmer gently for fifteen minutes. Drain, remove the outer skin, and mash fine. Make a white sauce, add the roes gradually to it, boil it up once, and it is ready for use. Serve with baked shad.

Follow the above directions to the point where the recipe calls for a white sauce. Use one batch of the bechamel sauce given under Shad à la Touraine (recipe 13). Combine the bechamel and the mashed roe; then thin with ½ cup hot milk and ½-¾ cup white mushroom stock. The recipe for the stock is also given under recipe 13. Serve this with Shad à la Touraine instead of the bechamel sauce given in that recipe.

INDIAN STEW OF TOMATOES

⌈ 1897 ⌉

SOURCE: MAST, CROWELL & KIRKPATRICK.

Standard American Cook Book. *Springfield, O.: Crowell &*
Kirkpatrick, 1897, page 146.

ROUGHWOOD COLLECTION.

Recipe of Sarah Tyson Rorer (1849-1937), Principal of the Philadelphia Cooking
School.

We chose this recipe from this particular cookbook as an example of Mrs. Rorer's
extraordinary culinary diaspora—her influence was not just limited to the books
she authored. Rorer recipes appeared individually in magazines, newspapers, and
of course, in hundreds of compilations like this one.

The *Standard American Cook Book* was issued by the publishers of the *Farm and
Fireside Library,* a monthly magazine that was something of a *Reader's Digest* for
rural America. All of the recipes were contributed by leading lights in American
cookery, such as Paul Resal, chef at the White House; Louis Marche, chef of the
Burnet House in Cincinnati; Angeline M. Weaver of the Hyde School Kitchen in
Boston; Gesine Lemcke of the German-American Cooking College in Brooklyn;
and of course, Mrs. Rorer of Philadelphia. We have made no attempt to judge this
recipe in terms of Mrs. Rorer's "best" or "worst," but we do believe that it hints at
the innumerable inventive ways one can treat a dish of this kind, as for example, in
the emendations we have added parenthetically to her recipe. Otherwise, the
whole thing carries off a bit like gazpacho, in spite of its name.

Indian Stew of Tomatoes

Boil six smooth tomatoes, cut them into halves, and press out the seeds; put them into a saucepan, add

½ green pepper, chopped
1 teaspoonful of salt
1 teaspoonful of turmeric dissolved in a little cold water (we use 1 tsp. curry instead)
½ teaspoonful of pepper (we use ⅛ tsp. cayenne)
¼ teaspoonful of ginger (we use ½ tsp.)

Cover the tomatoes with stock. If you have chicken-bones, they may be added, and you may then use water. Cook slowly for one half hour (we suggest poaching 20-30 minutes and no more); see that the tomatoes are not robbed of their shape; when done, remove the bones, if you have used them, add one tablespoonful of lemon-juice, one tablespoonful of butter, and one tablespoonful of flour moistened in a little cold water; bring to the boiling-point, and serve. This is one of the daintiest ways of serving this vegetable.

Since Mrs. Rorer's directions are clear enough, we cannot improve her procedure, but for clarity's sake, it would be helpful to list the additional required ingredients:

2 cups chicken stock
1 tblsp. lemon juice (we use 2 tblsp.)
1 tblsp. butter

1 tblsp. flour
(we also use 1-4 tblsp. sugar, depending on the tomatoes)

NOTE: After testing this recipe several times, we concluded that turmeric gave the dish an unpleasant metallic flavor, so we have suggested curry instead. We also feel that sugar will help enhance the flavor of the tomatoes.

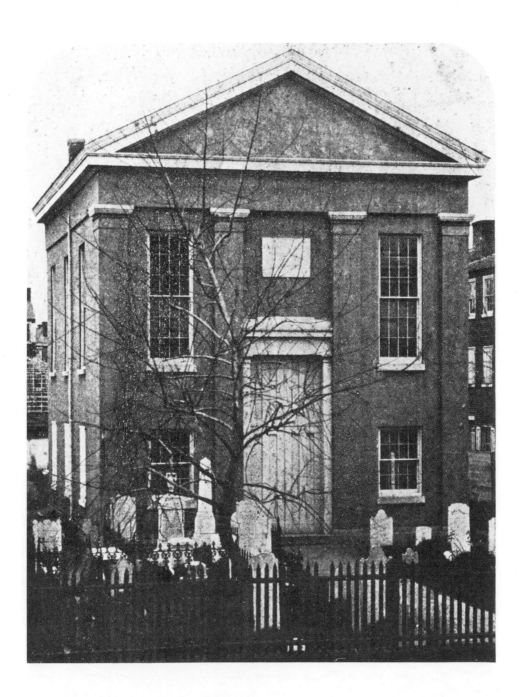

32. *The Bible Christian Church, Third Street above Girard. Erected in 1845 to replace an earlier wooden building, the church and property were sold in 1921 when the congregation declined. Once a center of vegetarian activism, the site was subsequently cleared to make way for a slaughter house. Illustration from* History of the Philadelphia Bible-Christian Church *(Philadelphia, 1922) p. 42.*

32

LEEK SOUP

⌈ 1906 ⌉

SOURCE: BENJAMIN SMITH LYMAN.

Vegetarian Diet and Dishes. *Philadelphia: Ferris & Leach,*
1917, page 203.

HISTORICAL SOCIETY OF PENNSYLVANIA.

Recipe of Maria Parloa (1843-1909), as published in Farmers' Bulletin No. 256
Preparation of Vegetables for the Table *(Washington, D.C.: Government Printing*
Office, 1906). Library Company of Philadelphia.

One of the most fascinating sidelights in the history of American diet is the Bible
Christian Church of Philadelphia, which became a focal point of the vegetarian
movement and dietary reform in the United States between 1817 and 1921. The
Bible Christians acted as a synthesis and watershed for new and sometimes radical
ideas, from the first attempts at canning vegetables by the North American Phalanx
in Monmouth County, New Jersey to health cereals from Battle Creek, Michigan.
Benjamin Smith Lyman (1835-1920) was influenced by Bible Christian
philosophies, particularly the emphasis on vegetarianism, and was thus inspired to
compile the first American vegetarian cookbook based on material drawn from a
broad array of sources — including Miss Parloa's government bulletin. He was
certainly one of the first American vegetarians to publish recipes for many Oriental
meat substitutes, including tofu, bean curd, and similar foods now common on the
health food and vegetarian market. We have selected the leek soup recipe from his
book not only because it has an impeccable pedigree coming as it does from Miss
Parloa, but also because it should quickly dispel any notions that old-fashioned
vegetarian soups lack flavor, interest, or style. Best of all, for those who must have
a low salt or low cholesterol diet, this soup may be indulged in without guilt!

Leek Soup

Wash the leeks, and cut off the roots. Cut the white part in thin slices.
Pare the potatoes and cut in dice. Put them in a bowl of cold water. Put
the butter, leeks, and onion in the soup pot and on the fire. Cook twenty
minutes slowly, stirring frequently, then add the hot water, potatoes, and
seasoning, and cook at least half an hour longer. Serve very hot. If it is
convenient and liked, cook with the leeks and butter the white stalks of 4
or 5 cibols, or 1 shallot may be cut fine and cooked with the leeks.

This is a delicious and wholesome soup, and is even better reheated the
second day than the first.

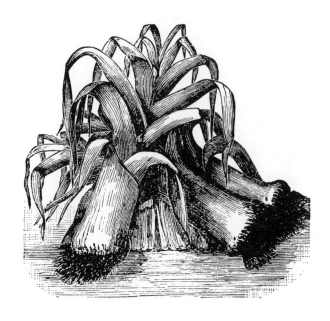

Since these directions are already clear, we cannot improve upon the recipe except to list the ingredients.

2 cups sliced leek (white part only)
4 cups diced potato
enough water to cover
2 tblsp. butter
4 tblsp. olive oil

4 tblsp. minced onion
3 qt. boiling water
3 tsp. salt
½ tsp. white pepper
1 shallot minced

NOTE: The flavor can be made more complex with the addition of potherbs. We suggest three from a list of herbs provided in Martha Brotherton's Bible Christian cookbook called *Vegetarian Cookery* (London, 1829).

2 tsp basil
4 tsp. parsley
½ tsp. tarragon

Pick the herbs fresh and mince them fine.

33

LUCKNOW SAUCE

SOURCE: The Madras Cookery Book for the People, by an Old Lady Resident. Fifth Edition—Revised and enlarged. *Madras and Bangalore: Higginbotham & Co., 1907, pages 73-74.*

COLLECTION OF VALERIE MARS, LONDON, ENGLAND.

Our recipe for Lucknow Sauce, a form of chutney, has a fascinating story behind it, which, if nothing else, should highlight the gulf that once existed between what was actually being consumed and what was recorded in cookbooks during the same period. We discovered that Lucknow Sauce was once quite popular in Philadelphia —the Merchant's Hotel featured it regularly on its menus in the 1870s—yet we could not locate a recipe in an American source. Not to have our curiosity defeated, a query about Lucknow Sauce was published in *Petits Propos Culinaires 19* (London, 1985).[1] Within a few months, our query was graciously answered by Valerie Mars, an English reader who supplied us with the recipe as published in *The Madras Cookery Book*.[2] Since *The Madras Cookery Book* first appeared in 1874, we were suddenly conscious of how up-to-date the kitchen of the Merchant's Hotel must have been. A few months later, the Lucknow connection was completed during a visit to the Gastronomy Museum in Vevey, Switzerland, where we discovered on permanent display one of the dragon-ornamented pots in which the sauce was exported. Thus, Lucknow Sauce reached Philadelphia via a china pot or an exotic cookbook. The last step, of course, was to make it ourselves—a complex undertaking that is now made easier with the food processor, and we might add, well worth the effort.

Lucknow Chatney

Limes 2 seers; sugar ½ seer; raisins or plums ½ seer; chillies, ginger, garlic, salt, each ¼ seer; vinegar, ¾ of a bottle.

Quarter the limes and soak them in the salt for three days, putting them daily in the sun and mixing; on the second day soak the raisins, chillies, ginger, and garlic in a little vinegar; the next day grind to a paste, remove the seeds, and pound the limes in a marble mortar to a pulp, mix well with the ground stuff and sugar, adding just enough vinegar to make it into a thick chatney.

Care should be taken not to touch with the hand when grinding, etc., use wooden spoons, as pickles touched spoil soon.

---

[1] William Woys Weaver, "Hydropathic Pudding and Lucknow Sauce," *Petits Propos Culinaires 19* (London, 1985), p. 61.

[2] Valerie Mars, "Lucknow Sauce," *Petits Propos Culinaires 21* (London, 1985), p. 69.

With the help of the British Museum, the old Bengali measures have been converted to standard American weights. We have also altered the procedure slightly, since Americans do not use the sun (as the Indians do) to cook or sterilize pickles.

North Fourth Street, Philadelphia.

5 lb. limes
1 lb. 4 oz. brown sugar
1 lb. 4 oz. raisins or prunes
1 lb. 4 oz. green peppers, chopped,
    plus ¾ cup chili powder
1 lb. 4 oz. garlic
1 lb. 4 oz. fresh ginger root, peeled
    and chopped
6 cups vinegar
1 cup pickling salt

Wash and quarter the limes. Put them in a deep crock and mix thoroughly with half the salt (½ cup). Stand for three days, stirring up the limes each day. On the third day, drain off the liquid, but do not rinse the limes.

In the meantime, on the second day, put the raisins or prunes, peppers, garlic, and ginger in a preserving kettle and stew in the vinegar for 25 minutes. (It is best to heat the vinegar separately, boil it five minutes, then pour it over the ingredients and proceed from there.) After cooking the ingredients, cool and cover.

On the third day, remove the seeds from the limes and grind the limes to a coarse paste. Grind the pepper, garlic, and ginger mixture also and mix everything together. (This can be done in a large food processor.) Add the remaining ½ cup of pickling salt.

Put the Lucknow Sauce in a large preserving kettle and boil for 40 minutes, stirring it often to keep it from scorching. If the mixture does not cook down to a smooth, creamy consistency, then reprocess until this consistency is achieved—it should have the final texture of smooth apple sauce. If the mixture has been reprocessed, then reheat it and boil five minutes. Add the chili powder and cook an additional five minutes. (Boiling water may be added if the mixture becomes too thick.) Pack in sterilized jars, seal, and give it a water bath of 15 minutes. Yield: 8-10 pints.

NOTE: Lucknow Sauce is best if allowed to mellow one month before using. Excellent with fish or fowl.

34

ROSICRUCIAN CHILI

[1917]

SOURCE: CLARA WITT.

The Rose Cross Aid Cook Book . . . *As authorized by*

R. *Swinburne Clymer, President of the Rose Cross Aid.*

Quakertown, Pa.: Printed at "Beverly Hall," 1917, page 76.

ROUGHWOOD COLLECTION.

R. Swinburne Clymer (1878-1967) was a physician who became the spiritual leader of the Rosicrucians in Pennsylvania and channeled much of his energy into dietary reform. He wrote numerous tracts and books on mysticism and health, among them, *Dietetics* (1917) and *Diet, The Way to Health* (1919). In all of his works, Clymer promoted plain food as opposed to *haute cuisine* and a dietary regime based on various "proper" nutrient combinations. Clymer saw these combinations as cornerstones to the successful diet; otherwise, incorrect combinations would lead to "inharmonious chemical reactions" which he translated directly into licentiousness and moral irresponsibility. In short, like Mrs. Horace Mann and her *Christianity in the Kitchen* (1857), Clymer made direct links between diet and morality. This is the overriding theme in all of his writings.

Since we wanted to include an example of a recipe illustrating the degree to which religious or philosophical thought could become entwined with cookery, we became increasingly impressed with Mrs. Witt's chili. As an adherent of Clymer's teachings and the wife of a Rosicrucian minister in Kansas City, she imbued her recipes with orthodox Clymerism.

Our Rosicrucian chili is *chili con carne* without the *carne*, easy enough to explain when we understand that Clymer wrote: "One of the prime causes of cancer is the eating of meat."[1] From a Rosicrucian standpoint this chili is therefore free of those inharmonious chemical reactions ever lurking in the pot—well, almost. It turns out that beans are extremely dangerous. To quote Clymer again: "Dried beans in any form, especially baked with bacon or ham, with beer as a drink, and served with bread or potatoes are destructive to clean thoughts and habits, clean life, health and peace."[2] Beans, it is true, are notoriously destructive of one's inner peace, but in the hands of the overzealous chef, Clymer concluded that they become nothing less than an instrument of murderous melancholy, unchecked passion, solitary vices, and other spice cabinet pitfalls.

---

[1]R. Swinburne Clymer, *Diet, The Way to Health* (Quakertown, Pa., 1919), p. 304.
[2]*Ibid.*, p. 109.

We found the recipe a bit anticlimactic. We cannot guarantee that our suggested emendations will serve as a protection from any of the above pitfalls, but after testing the chili many times over, each time in ardent expectation of rising chemicals, uncheckable passions, etc., we can only report that as far as we know, nothing much happened.

Vegetarian Chili

Soak a pound of chili beans or kidney beans over night. Cook until tender. Add an onion browned in two tablespoons of olive oil, one cup of tomatoes and a small can of salmon. Season highly with red pepper, add salt and cook for another hour, this should not be dry but rather loose and served in sauce dishes. Mexican beans can be used if preferred.

1 lb. chili beans	2 cups boiling water

Cover the beans as directed and let stand overnight. Drain and cook tender in 5 cups of water.

Then add:

1 cup fresh tomato, seeded and ground up	1 tsp. cayenne pepper
1 lb. canned salmon, cleaned of skin and bones	2 cups chopped onion fried in 2 tblsp. olive oil
	1 tsp. salt

Suggested Options:

Use 3 cups tomato juice plus 2 cups water instead of 5 cups water in which to cook the beans. Remove 3 cups cooked beans with liquid and puree; return this to the pot and proceed by adding the tomato, salmon, etc. Season with:

4 tblsp. dark brown sugar	1 tsp. minced fresh coriander leaves
1 tsp. minced garlic	1 tsp. minced parsley

35

DANDELION AND SCALLION SALAD
[1921]

SOURCE: ANNA B. SCOTT.

Mrs. Scott's North American Seasonal Cook Book.

Philadelphia: John C. Winston Co., 1921, page 29.

ROUGHWOOD COLLECTION.

Recipe of Anna B. Scott, food columnist for the Philadelphia North American *and later for the* Philadelphia Inquirer.

We wanted to include a recipe from an early Philadelphia food columnist. Mrs. Scott's work is both typical of that genre and historically important. She is believed to have been the first daily newspaper food columnist in the United States, a claim that may require qualification, since many Philadelphia papers, beginning in the 1840s, carried regular "departments" on the home and kitchen, often overseen by the editor's wife. In any event, Mrs. Scott was quite influential nationally. She wrote about trends, she chose recipes that would appeal to her readers, and, from time to time, she published collections of recipes. Illustrated here is her 32-page cookbook issued in 1936 as a supplement to the *Philadelphia Inquirer*.[1] Incidentally, that is not Mrs. Scott on the cover.

Her dandelion and scallion salad is a forthright country dish that doubtless appealed to Pennsylvania-Dutch and Italian-American readers. Nutritionally, dandelion is far richer in good things than lettuce, but certainly, lettuce may be substituted when dandelion is not available.

---

[1] See Elaine Tait, "Vintage Recipes Yield Sweet Nostalgia," *Philadelphia Inquirer*, Nov. 3, 1982.

The Philadelphia Inquirer
PUBLIC LEDGER
Supplement to the Philadelphia Inquirer, November 15, 1936

COOK BOOK

by

MRS. ANNA B. SCOTT

Dandelion and Scallion Salad

Clean, wash and cut the dandelion into ½ inch pieces, scallions are cut the same. Put into cold water for 1 hour; drain; put into a flour bag that you keep for that purpose. The egg is made the day before. A good plan is to make enough salad dressing for a week. When mealtime comes, mix dandelion, scallions and dressing together, and garnish with finely chopped hard boiled egg.

Mrs. Scott's directions need no improvement, but we think the following will help clarify her quantities:

1 qt. berry box dandelion leaves (measure after cutting up)
1 cup cut scallion
½ cup dressing (see recipe 19.)
1 hard boiled egg

NOTE: The dandelion is soaked in water to remove bitterness. The flour bag she mentions is an old technique for removing excess moisture and for keeping lettuce crisp while it stands in a wooden bowl on a block of ice—she is presuming that her readers do not own refrigerators.

INDEX
(Numbers refer to recipe numbers)